NORTH LIGHT
GRAPHIC WORKBOOKS

Marker Techniques

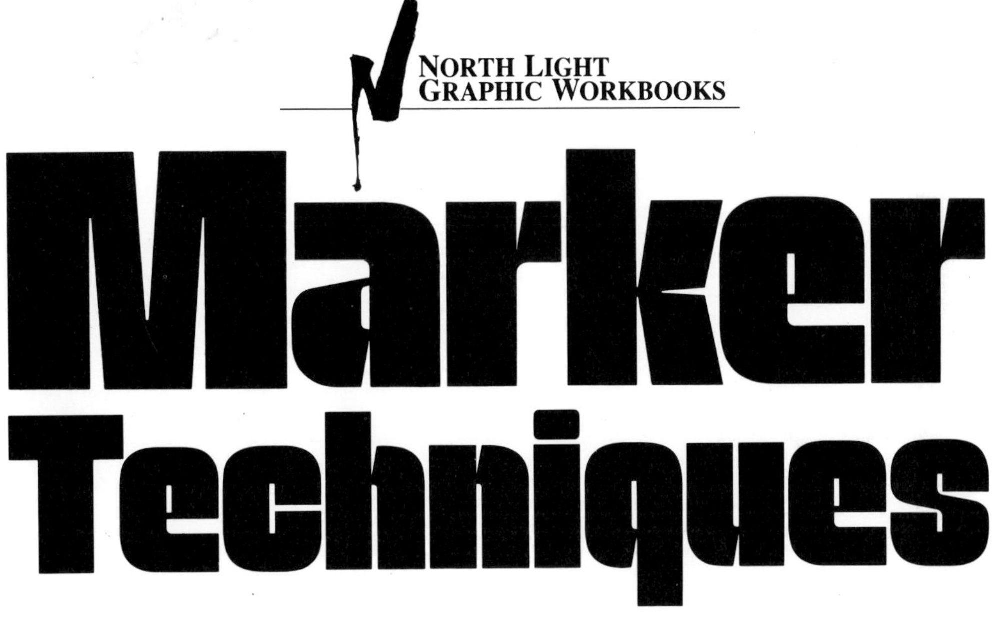

RENDERING REFLECTIVE SURFACES
WORKBOOK 2

Lee Woolery

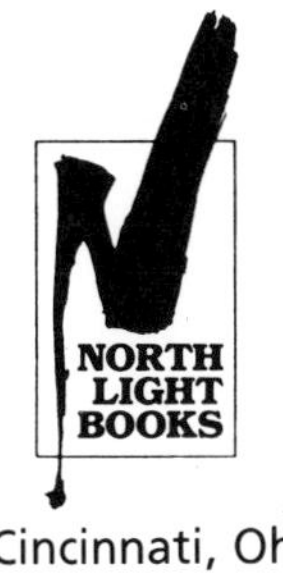

NORTH LIGHT BOOKS

Cincinnati, Ohio

Concept and editorial development by Diana Martin
Interior design by Carol Buchanan

INTRODUCTION

Product rendering is a mainstay of commercial art; products run the gamut from kitchen utensils to high-rise apartments. Successfully depicting a product hinges largely on your ability to capture the character of its surface. Professional illustrators know that a viewer, with just one look at the surface, should be able to tell whether a pair of roller skates are made of metal or plastic, or if a plate is of paper or china. If your surface rendering is accurate, that single glance should tell volumes about a product.

Any shrewd product designer can tell you that reflective materials always catch the customer's eye, which makes them an invaluable sales tool. As an illustrator, you must be able to capture these surface characteristics on paper. Specifically, you'll have to know how to render plastic, glass, and chrome—the three most popular reflective materials in commercial use.

Each has a shiny boldness, yet each is unique. Certain rendering techniques, such as glazing, carry over from one material to another, yet proficient artists know how to modify these to fit their subjects. They know how to use a marker in ways that ''say'' plastic, glass, or chrome. With this workbook, and throughout the *Marker Techniques* series, you'll learn how to become one of those skilled artists.

The Workbook

The workbook is a wonderful teaching and learning method. You'll be actively participating by doing projects and be guided simultaneously by step-by-step demonstrations and instructional captions. Through dedicated practice, you can acquire skill and confidence at a rapid pace.

Each workbook in the *Marker Techniques* series is designed to take you one step at a time, so that the information and skills that you learn in the very first project can be incorporated into the successful completion of the second project, the third, and so on. The information and skills that you ac-

quire will work like building blocks to help you achieve your goal of doing professional marker rendering.

As you look through the workbook you'll notice that at the beginning of each project there's an explanation of the challenges the project presents and the techniques you'll learn for mastering them. Next comes a step-by-step demonstration that shows you the mechanics of each technique, as well as the way different rendering methods can be combined. Following the last demonstration you'll find multiple practice pages for each project where the drawings' outlines have been preprinted. Some have guidelines for you to follow that indicate contour areas, highlights, shadows, and/or details. These should help you capture an object's unique look, but remember, your rendering technique is what will really give it a realistic appearance.

Reflective Surfaces

Rendering Reflective Surfaces is the second in the *Marker Techniques* series of four workbooks. This workbook will teach you how to successfully render plastic, chrome, and glass surfaces with art markers.

You will use rendering techniques taught in Workbook 1, *Basic Skills.* If you're unsure about how to fill in color, how to control bleed, or how to build tone with glazing, refer back to Workbook 1 before proceeding.

You'll begin by learning how to render plastic, which is used today in many high-tech products. Not all plastics are reflective, of course; some have surface textures that are downright dull. But many formulations, especially polyethylene, do have a slick shine and a distinctively reflective quality—that's the type of plastic you'll be concentrating on here.

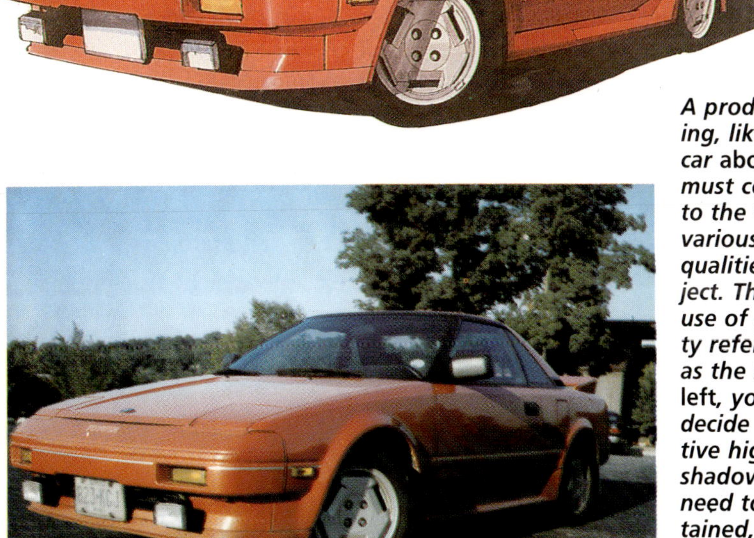

A product rendering, like that of the car above left, must communicate to the viewer the various surface qualities of the object. Through the use of good quality references such as the Polaroid, left, you can better decide what reflective highlights, shadows, or details need to be retained, eliminated, or embellished in order to show the product and its surfaces to their best advantage.

Highly reflective plastic surfaces share certain characteristics with painted surfaces: Both have rich, saturated color, and they reflect much of their surroundings. Plastic reflects shadows, as well as objects that are darker and lighter than its surface color. The rule of thumb with plastic is the shinier the surface, the more reflections will appear. You'll learn how to place marker strokes replicating these reflections without losing the plastic's bold color. To prepare yourself, study plastic objects to see how light and dark reflections look.

When it comes to rendering chrome, keep in mind that this material has no color of its own. Chrome reflects color from its surroundings, bouncing off everything in its view. The size and shape of chrome reflections depend on the object's configuration. You'll soon see this firsthand as you render a chrome cylinder; here, because the object is linear, reflections will appear as bands of color in light and dark values. In later workbooks you'll see how reflections will wrap around the shape of a chrome object, like a car bumper.

High contrast is another key characteristic of chrome. You'll see a white highlight somewhere, usually at the top, and dark shadows near the bottom or away from the light source. Darks may also come from a dark-valued object near the surface. Again, you should mentally prepare for this project by observing the way chrome reflects color, light, and shadow.

Glass is the most difficult reflective material to render because, unlike plastic or chrome, it is transparent. To capture this transparency, you must render not only the glass surface, but what's behind it.

Clear glass absorbs color from its surroundings, taking on their general tint. If the sun is at the proper angle, glass can be as reflective as a mirror. For the most part, however, glass bounces back white reflections that appear to be floating.

The position of a glass surface in your illustration will determine how you render it. If it's a windshield, for instance, you won't want to obscure the car's interior with a mass of white highlights. If,

on the other hand, you're rendering an office building, you don't want to needlessly show interior clutter through the windows. With experience you'll learn the best way to handle these rendering situations as they come up.

As with plastic and chrome, you should observe glass firsthand and in photographs to better understand how its different reflections look. There will be some guidelines on the practice pages to help you, but it still helps to understand ahead of time why something appears the way it does.

Your Next Marker Step

After completing Workbook 2, you can progress to Workbook 3, *Rendering Textured Surfaces,* which will teach you how to develop renderings with multiple textures, like bread and fruit on a wooden cutting board, or a concrete building framed by bushes and trees. The three projects in this workbook become progressively more complex as your level of expertise grows. The projects in Workbook 3 are very similar to the assignments encountered by professional illustrators.

Workbook 4, *Illustration,* challenges what you've learned in the three previous notebooks. Here you'll discover how to render subjects that look complicated—a rooster, a football action scene, an automobile—using a series of simple, systematic rendering techniques.

Professional Marker Rendering

Many situations in today's visual marketplace demand a quick means of portraying an image in color. A designer may have a great idea for a product, but she or he needs a way to show people what it will look like. A marker rendering is the perfect solution. Unlike a three-dimensional prototype or a full-blown illustration, a marker rendering can be done quickly and economically.

This type of assignment, and dozens of others like it, is generated every day in the graphic art world. With a portfolio of crisp marker renderings, your chances of finding a job with a studio or ad

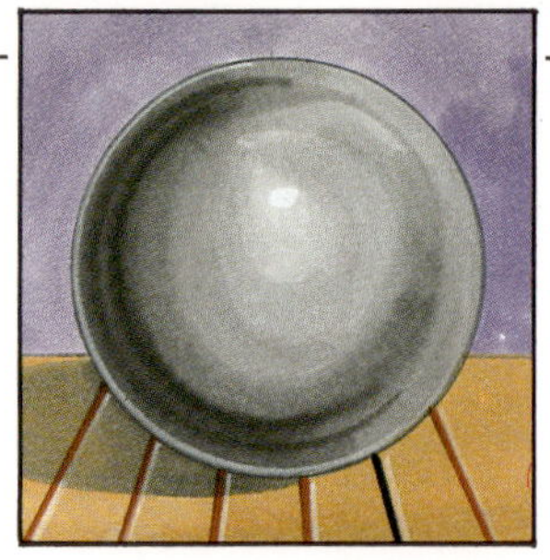

Metallic Surface

A

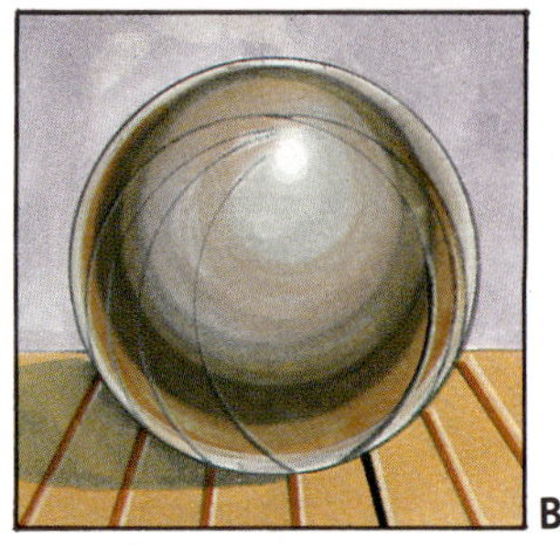

B

Metallic Surface

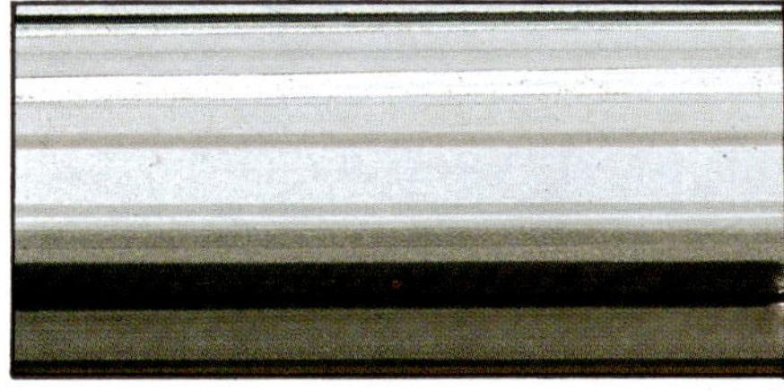

A

B

Painted Surface

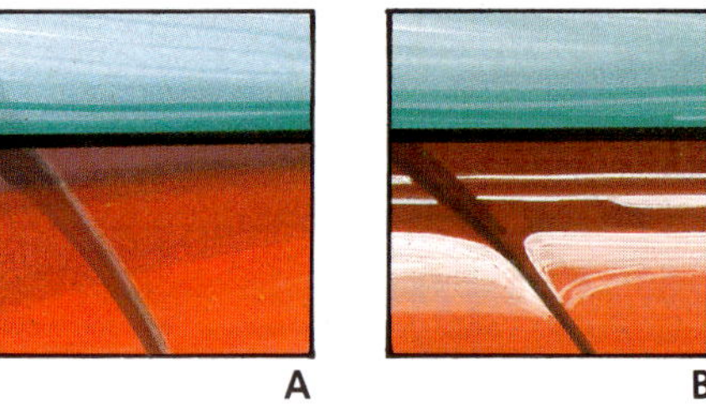

A   **B**

Transparent Surface

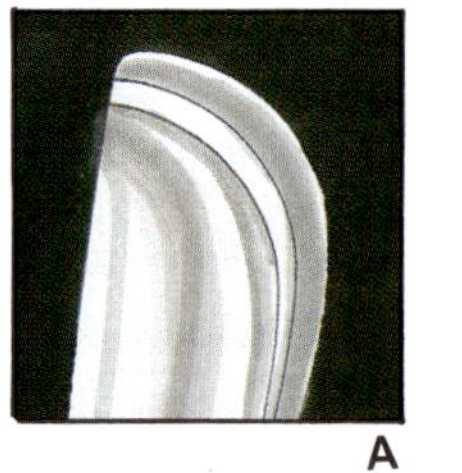

A   **B**

These eight examples show how reflections can make your renderings more exciting and dynamic. Examples A show only highlights and shadows. Examples B show not only lights and darks but reflected sky, background, and ground colors.

agency are excellent. Be sure your portfolio includes product renderings as well as loose sketches and more detailed studies. Don't be afraid to develop—or to show—your versatility!

Supplies You'll Need

Markers: For this workbook you'll need a full set of Berol Prismacolor double-nibbed cool gray markers ranging in tone from 10% to 80%, plus apple blossom, scarlet lake, magenta, cranberry, grape, non-photo blue, sand, brick white, and black. A Berol marker, with a nib on each end (one broad and the other fine), lets you render large areas and small without changing markers. Before buying your markers, review the section on selecting markers in Workbook 1.

Other Materials: To complete these three projects you'll need a white Prismacolor pencil, a straightedge, a no. 0 sable brush, Dr. Martin's Bleed Proof White paint, and 55- and 35-degree ellipse guides.

Work Space: Your drawing table should be large enough so that all of your supplies can be laid out within easy reach. It should also be well lit and well ventilated, since some marker fumes can be hazardous to your health.

Selecting Paper

Once you've completed this workbook you'll want to continue practicing on your own. The paper you choose to use is as important as your choice of marker. There are some twenty different brands of paper specially made for marker use. My choice is the Aquabee Series 633 marker paper because it retains the color's accuracy and keeps bleed to a minimum. Some papers will bleed a great deal but give you very accurate color. Others will bleed very little, but color is muted and almost pastel in intensity.

In my opinion, it's better to use a paper that bleeds but retains color intensity. You'll learn to control bleed much quicker with this paper. A paper that bleeds a great deal allows you more time to blend and glaze colors because it takes longer for the pigment to dry. The other type of paper will absorb the pigment too quickly, leaving hardly any time for blending. As you can see, the paper is an integral part of marker rendering. I would suggest choosing a paper the same way you would a marker: try a few samples at an art supply store to find the one that best suits your needs.

The practice paper provided in this workbook does allow some color to bleed through. Place a piece of ordinary typing paper beneath each practice page as you work. Also the Berol broad nib marker bleeds slightly more than the fine. You should keep the broad nib 1/16 inch away from the drawn lines and the fine nib 1/32 inch. Keep in mind that new markers bleed differently from old ones, bleed can vary from color to color, and nib pressure affects bleed.

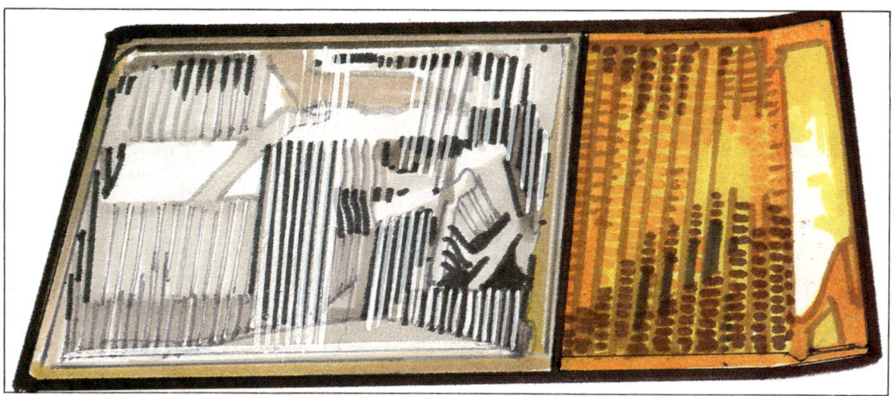

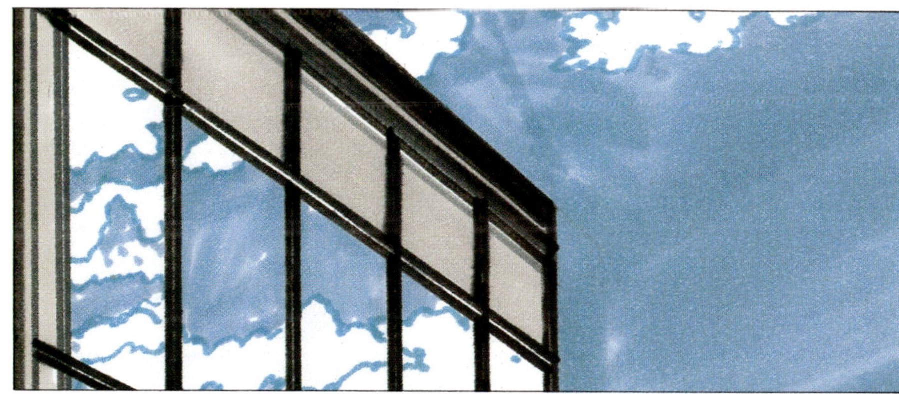

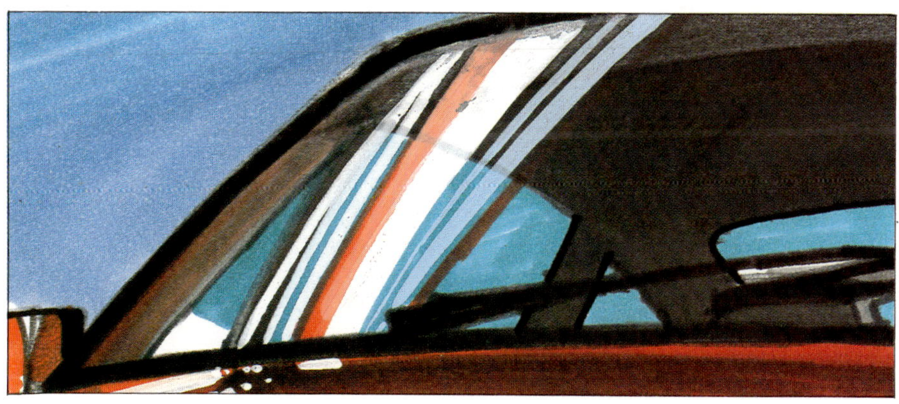

Glass is the most difficult material to render because of its transparency. In the headlamp assembly, **top,** *you see the textural pattern on the lens as well as the lights and darks inside. The rendering of the building,* middle, *shows the mirrorlike character of some window glass. On the car windshield,* above, *you can see its transparent and reflective nature.*

SLICK PLASTIC

Most plastic products are colored, so you're faced with the challenge of keeping color bright while still showing lights, darks, and shadows. This can be accomplished using the glazing method taught in Workbook 1. However, instead of using the grays, as you did in Workbook 1, here you'll substitute a color-keyed tonal "palette." Working from the lightest areas to the darkest, you'll build up reflections and form while developing saturated color.

This plastic wastebasket calls for five red-toned markers: apple blossom, scarlet lake, magenta, cranberry, and grape. The foot pedal and cast shadow will be rendered in cool gray; you'll need 20%, 40%, 50%, 60%, 70%, and 80% grays, plus black. Highlights will be sharpened with a white Prismacolor pencil.

Assemble your supplies and read through each step before starting. Pull out the full-page reproduction of this illustration that follows Project 3. Pay particular attention to the way lights and darks are reflected onto the top and sides. Notice, for example, that the cast shadow is reflected onto the shaded side of the can.

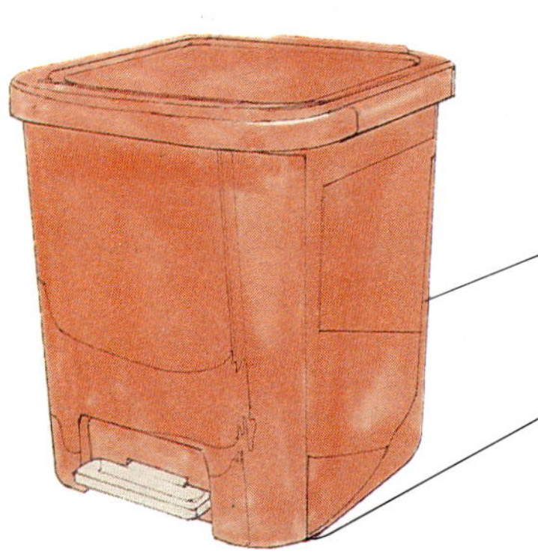

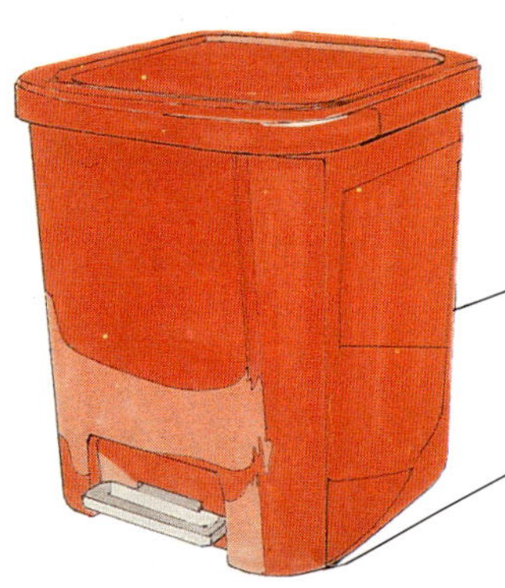

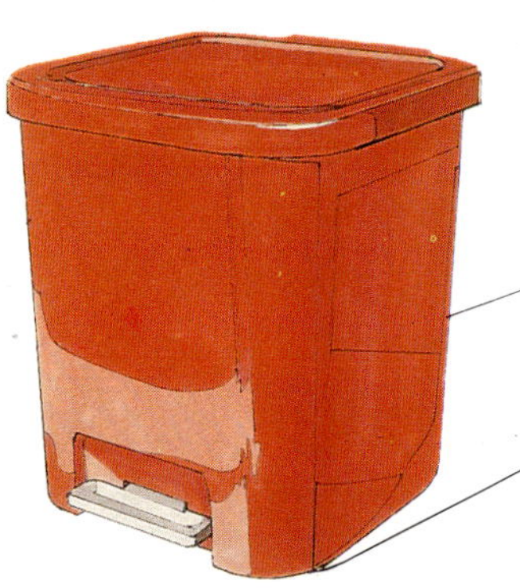

Step 1: 1) Guidelines for all the highlights, shadows, and reflections are indicated on the drawing. Study the final rendering to be sure you know which are which before beginning. 2) Using the broad nib, fill in the entire wastebasket with a layer of apple blossom. Leave the highlight on the lid white by drawing around it, working quickly to keep the color flat and even. Stay within the lines and don't let any color bleed into the pedal area. 3) Fill in the foot pedal with 20% gray. Use the fine point for this small area.

Step 2: 1) Apply scarlet lake all over the wastebasket except in the lightest front indentation areas that will stay apple blossom. Use the broad nib and be careful not to bleed into the apple blossom areas. 2) On the right side, in shadow, use *vertical* strokes of scarlet lake to enhance the wastebasket's structure. By carefully ruling the marker strokes with a little overlap, these will look like shiny streaks. 3) Darken the foot pedal, except for the light indentation, using the fine point of a 40% gray.

Step 3: 1) Add some 50% gray on the shadow side of the pedal with a fine point, then some black where it goes inside the can. 2) Apply magenta to the shaded side of the can using vertical strokes as you did in Step 2. When you've completed the side, add magenta above the foot pedal and around the edges on the can's top with the fine point using strokes that will enhance the form. 3) Next, apply some strokes of cranberry to the shaded side of the lid and the indentation on top of it using the fine point.

Step 4: 1) Intensify the areas of pure apple blossom by stroking on another layer of it using your fine point. Be sure this pale marker doesn't touch any darker surroundings, or they'll stain your nib. 2) Fill in the cast shadow with a 60% gray. Use the fine point around the can, then switch to the broad nib as the shadow pulls away. The fine point not only gives you more control near the can but also covers better, thereby creating a more intense shadow where it falls closest to the object. 3) Using the fine point of your cranberry marker, fill in the reflections on the shaded side of the can. Keep using vertical strokes that reinforce its vertical form.

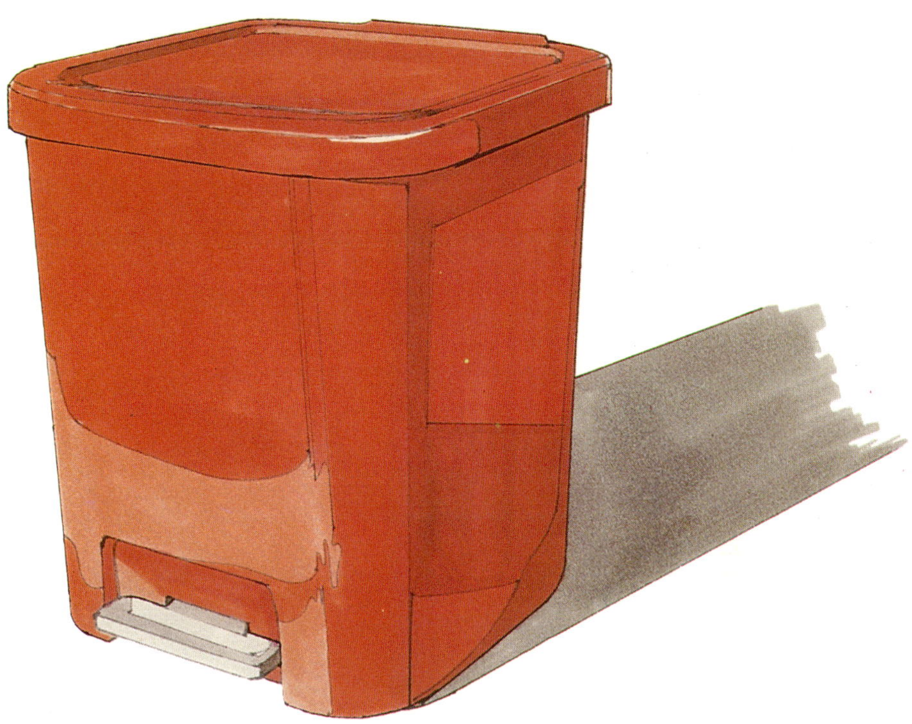

Step 5: 1) Fill in the front edge of the cast shadow using the fine point of a 70% gray. While it's still wet, glaze over this layer with the broad nib of a 60% gray to give a smoother transition between tones. 2) Give the can's shaded side another layer of fine, vertical cranberry strokes, then run another layer of apple blossom over all areas still that color. 3) At the very front of the cast shadow, where it slips under the can, apply some 80% gray using a fine point. Next, cover the foot pedal with a light layer of 40% gray using the fine point. 4) Apply fine accents of grape to the darkest red areas on the wastebasket's shaded side, its lid, and top indentation. This will heighten the deep red cast, giving the can a three-dimensional form. 5) Add another layer of scarlet lake to the lighted side and top of the can to increase overall color intensity, but don't bleed into the apple blossom areas. 6) With the white pencil, draw around and through the existing highlight on the lid, then gently pull a fine white line off it to bolster the reflection.

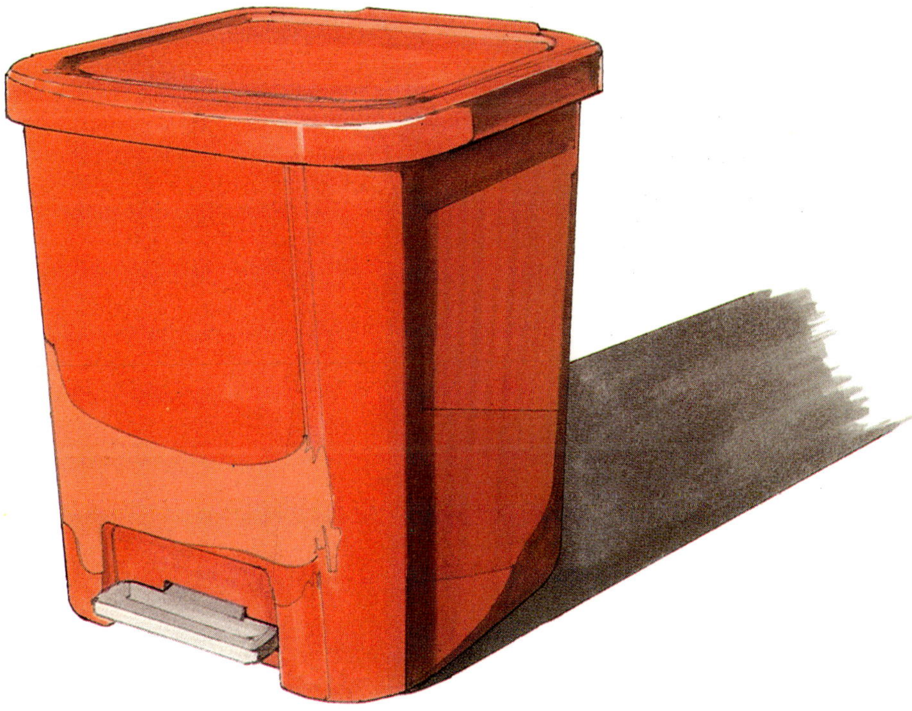

SHINY CHROME

Chrome is the most reflective of surfaces. Unlike plastic, chrome has no color of its own—all of its "color" is reflected from surrounding objects.

On a chrome cylinder the reflections appear as bars running lengthwise. For simplicity, this project calls for you to use shades of light blue at the top, to show reflected sky, and earth tones at the bottom, to indicate color from the ground. A chrome cylinder also has a white highlight bar and a black shadow bar.

Step 1: 1) Stroke 10% gray along the bottom third and very top of the cylinder; then use this marker to fill in the end. You may do the reflective bands freehand, but stroking along a straightedge will give a better reflective effect. Because the object is both linear and metallic, these lines need to be as sharp as possible. 2) When the end dries, add some 20% gray near the edge by stroking along the inside of a 35-degree ellipse.

Step 2: 1) Use your straightedge and nonphoto blue marker to draw color bands of sky reflections. Place one band at the top and another midway down. 2) With the fine point and the 35-degree ellipse, add blue to either end. 3) Apply the sand marker across the very bottom using a straightedge and to the cylinder's end using a 35-degree ellipse to indicate curved form.

Step 3: 1) Lay 50% gray along the bottom, below the midpoint blue, and near the top. When these dry, put another layer over the lower midpoint gray band. 2) Fill in shapes on the cylinder's end with 50% gray. 3) Stroke two bands of blue beneath the top gray stripe; let dry. Add another layer of blue to the bottom band. 4) Blend the edge between the white highlight strip and the blue band directly above it by running your brick white marker over it.

To capture the look of chrome, all the colors have to be clean, rich, and bright. You'll accomplish this with glazing and blending. The difference between these two techniques is that blending requires you go over two glazed values with the lighter valued one to soften the contrast between two areas. By creating a smoother transition, you enhance the object's three-dimensional appearance.

For this project you'll need brick white, nonphoto blue, sand, and black markers, plus cool grays in tones of 10%, 20%, 40%, 50%, 60%, and 70%. You'll also need a straightedge, a white Prismacolor pencil, plus 55-degree and 35-degree ellipse guides. With this rendering you'll be using the fine points of your markers exclusively. The fine point works best for this type of glazing because you can build lines as wide as you need them. A full-page reproduction of this illustration follows Project 3.

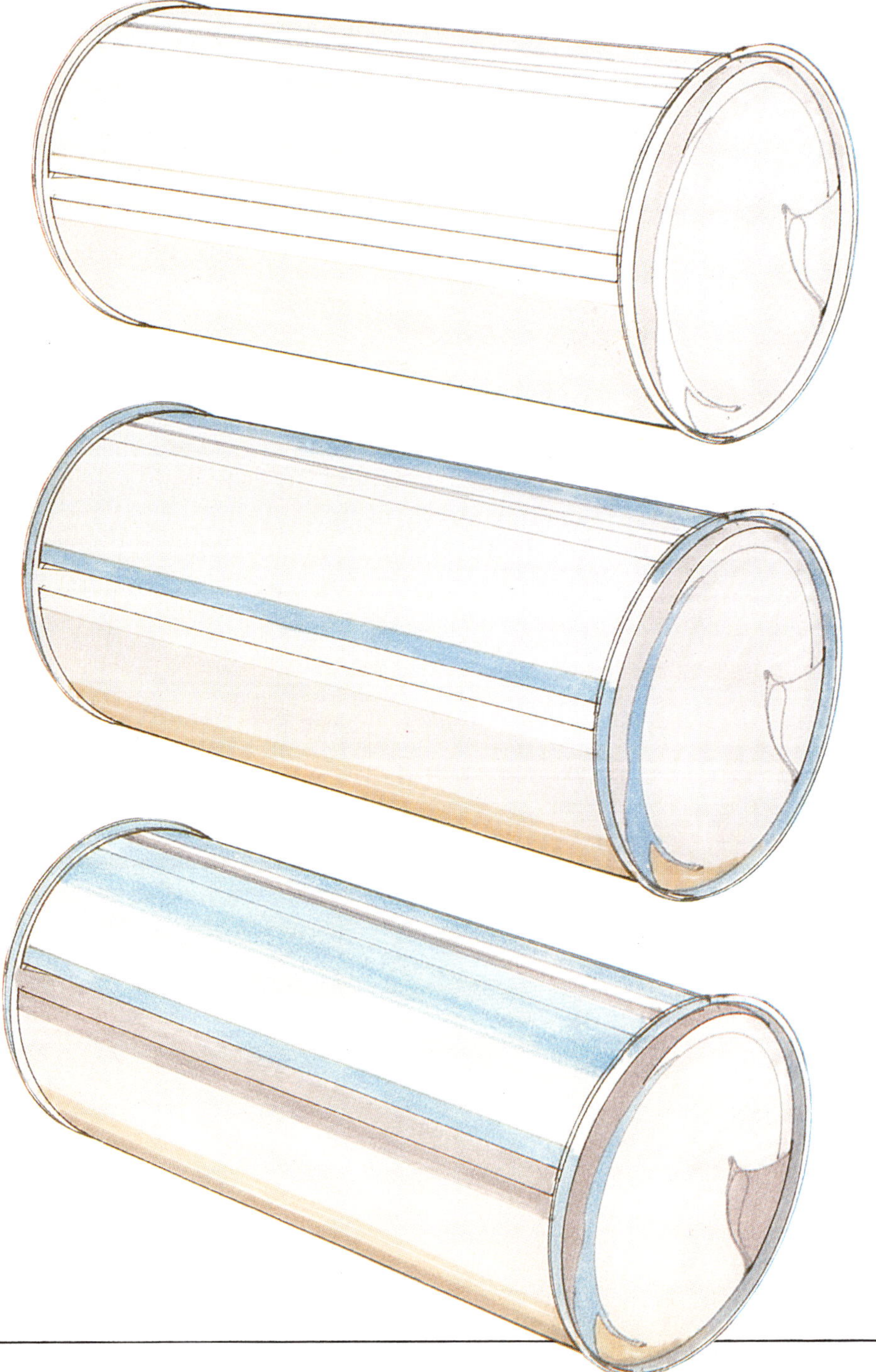

Step 4: 1) Fill in the end of the cylinder using a 40% gray marker. Keeping the gray out of the blue and sand areas, apply strokes with the fine point that connote the shape's roundness. Leave some reflective highlights uncovered, as seen in the example. 2) When the 40% gray dries, apply 60% gray to the curved lip and dark indentation on the cylinder's end. 3) Using the straightedge, run a line of 60% gray across the middle of the cylinder, making sure you stop at the ellipse edge.

Step 5: 1) Outline the inside of the rear edge using a 55-degree ellipse guide and the fine nib of the black marker. 2) Using the straightedge, draw black lines across the middle of the cylinder to create contrast. (These lines go over the preexisting gray.) 3) Stroke a series of 50% gray lines on the bottom half of the cylinder to further model its form. Working wet-over-wet, rule your lines so that there's a bit of an overlap; again, this helps create the look of shimmering chrome. 4) Apply a band of 30% gray at the very top of the cylinder to neutralize the blue.

Step 6: 1) Run a fine line of 50% gray around the outside edge of the front end using the 35-degree ellipse guide. 2) With the fine nib of the black marker and that same ellipse, stroke around the inside edge of the front lip. 3) Using your straightedge, stroke a 70% gray band directly below the black line in the middle. Then, to give the cylinder a complete form, run a line of 70% gray across the bottom and the top. 4) Clean up any minor bleed marks along the front end by stroking over them with the white Prismacolor pencil. Place your 35-degree ellipse guide on the edge, then stroke the pencil along it for a sharp edge.

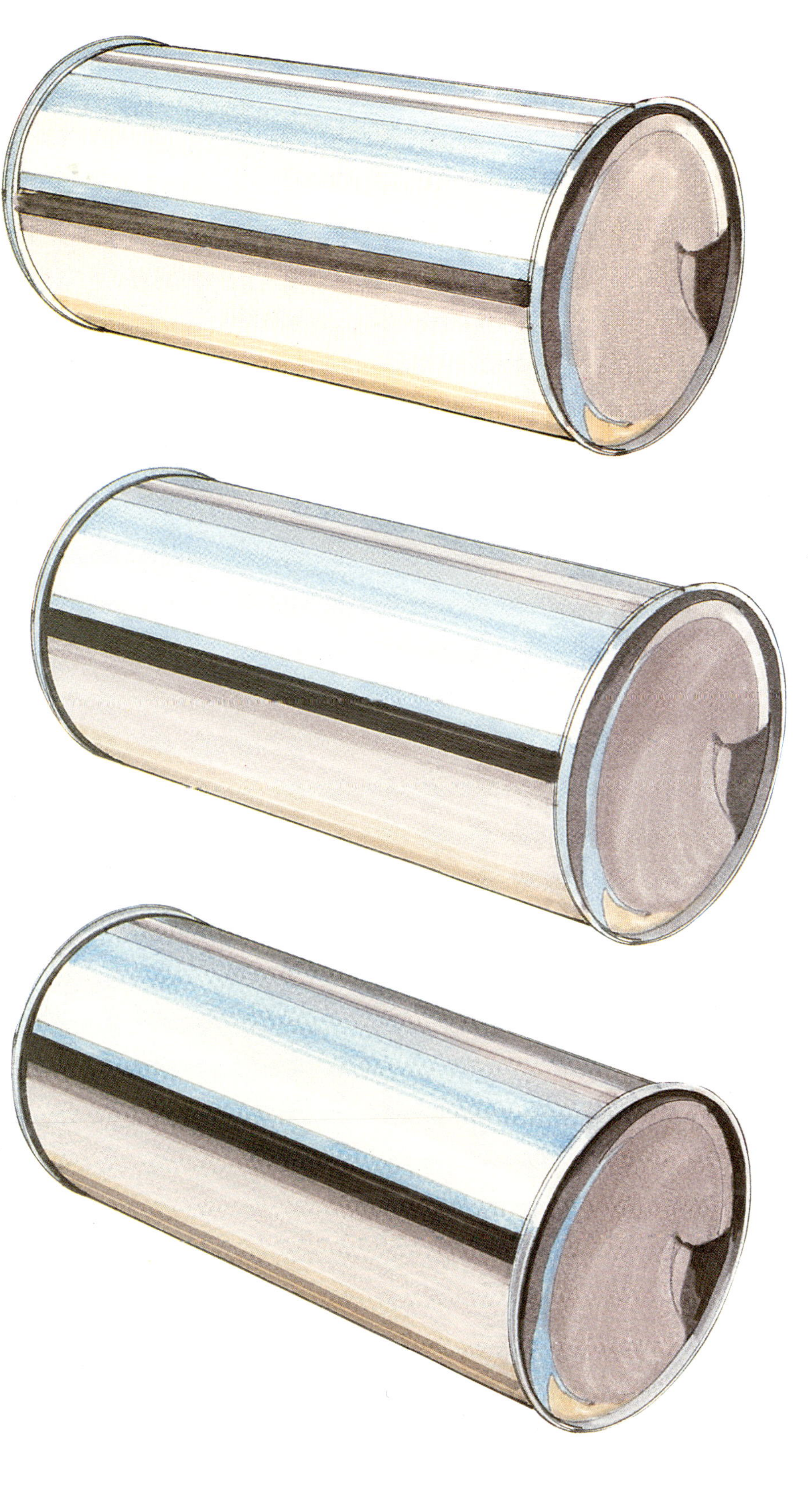

TRANSPARENT GLASS

Glass is this workbook's last reflective surface because it is the most difficult. Since glass is transparent; you must render what is behind it, as well as its reflections. Yet despite this added difficulty, glass is rendered like any other reflective surface: you will glaze and slowly build up reflections, creating the look of transparency by allowing layers to show through.

Before you can realistically render glass, you have to understand its unique characteristics. Sharp reflections on glass are white. These flashes of white appear to be floating, a look that's enhanced when they're ren-dered with hard and soft edges. Clear glass also has its dark areas. They'll appear farthest away from the light, at the bottom of a glass, or near a handle, for instance. Glass absorbs color. Rather than bouncing back distinct colors, it reflects more subtle tints. Colors appear in the same areas as darks, since both are absorbed from the surroundings. The thickness and structure of the glass will also dictate where darks and color appear.

For this project you'll need cool gray markers ranging in tone from 20% to 70%, plus sand, nonphoto blue, brick white, and black markers. You'll also need Dr. Martin's Bleed Proof White paint and a no. 0 sable brush.

Carefully study each step before you start this rendering. A full-page reproduction of this illustration follows the last step. As you glaze these very light shades of cool grays, you must keep them from getting too dark too soon. Rendering glass takes patience because the value shifts are so subtle. Don't get frustrated if it takes several attempts before you get the results you want. Once you've successfully completed this project, move on to the more complex challenges in Workbook 3, *Rendering Textured Surfaces.*

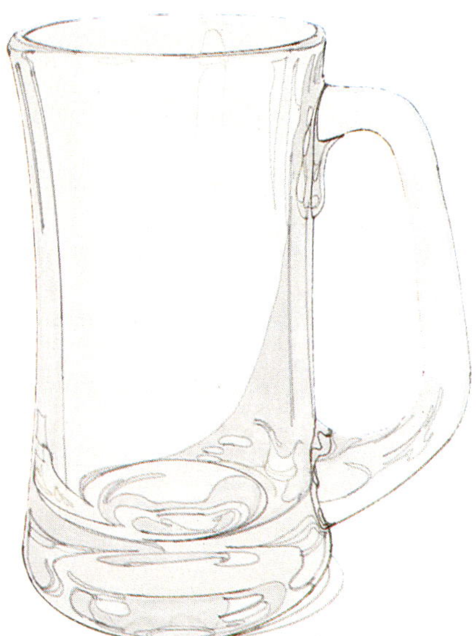 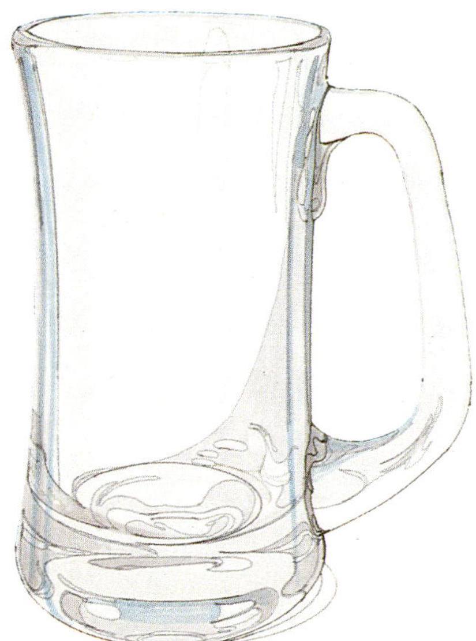 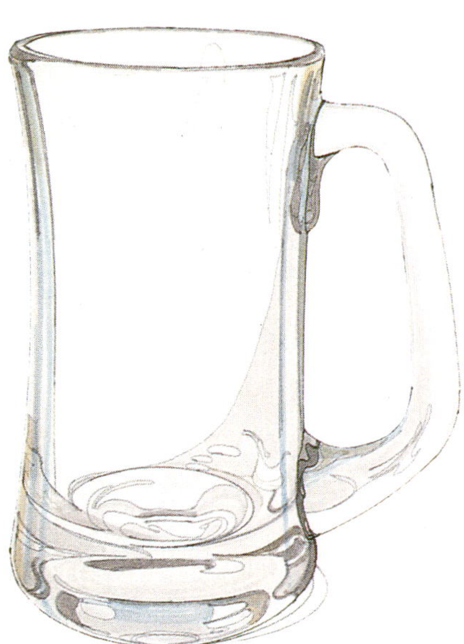

Step 1: 1) Cover the entire glass—except for highlights indicated on the drawing—with brick white. Apply vertical strokes that follow the glass's form using the broad nib. When this dries, take the fine point and apply another layer to the inside of the handle, the inner shadow shape falling from the upper right-hand corner, and the bottom. 2) With the fine point, place another layer of brick white along the left side, inside the mug's opening, and over the handle. Remember, these areas must be built up slowly to create a transparent look. 3) Stroke 20% gray around the lip of the glass, along the left side, and inside the handle with the fine point. Lightly fill in the diagonal shadow shape on the right.

Step 2: 1) Add some reflected color to the left side with the fine point of a nonphoto blue, following the glass's contour. Then add blue to the bottom (near the middle) and along the right side into the handle. 2) Using the fine point, apply 30% gray around the entire bottom, along the handle, and around the lip. Watch for bleeding in areas, such as these, where you have a value contrast. The break in tone must be sharp to look realistic.

Step 3: 1) To give the handle form, add 20% gray to the inside and the very top with your fine point. 2) Take the fine point of your sand marker and put some color around the top corners, on the handle, and along the bottom left and middle. 3) Begin adding darks to the glass using the fine point of a 60% gray. Stroke around the lip, where the handle joins the glass, and inside the reflective shapes at the bottom. Run two lines of 60% gray that follow the glass's contour along the upper left side.

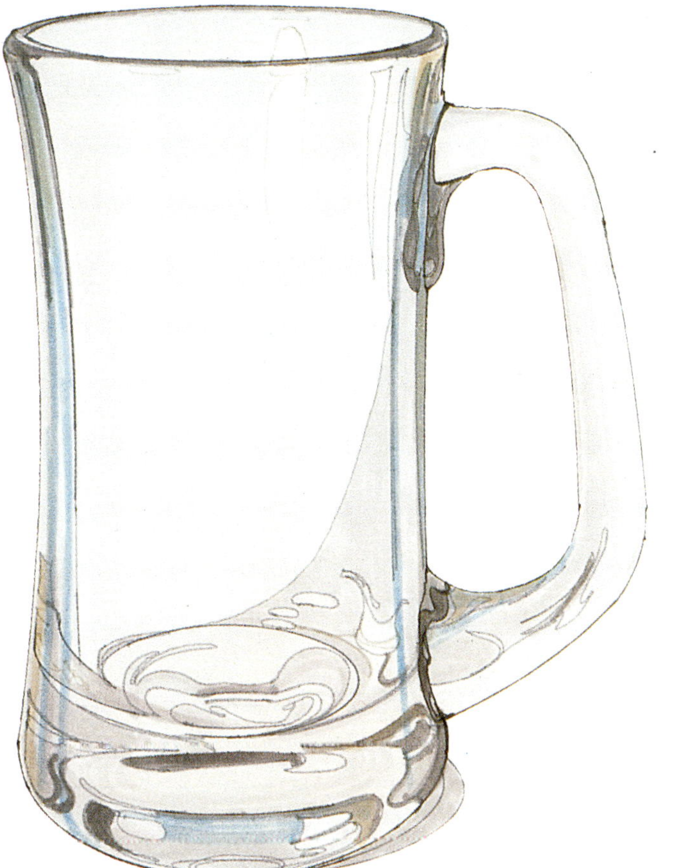 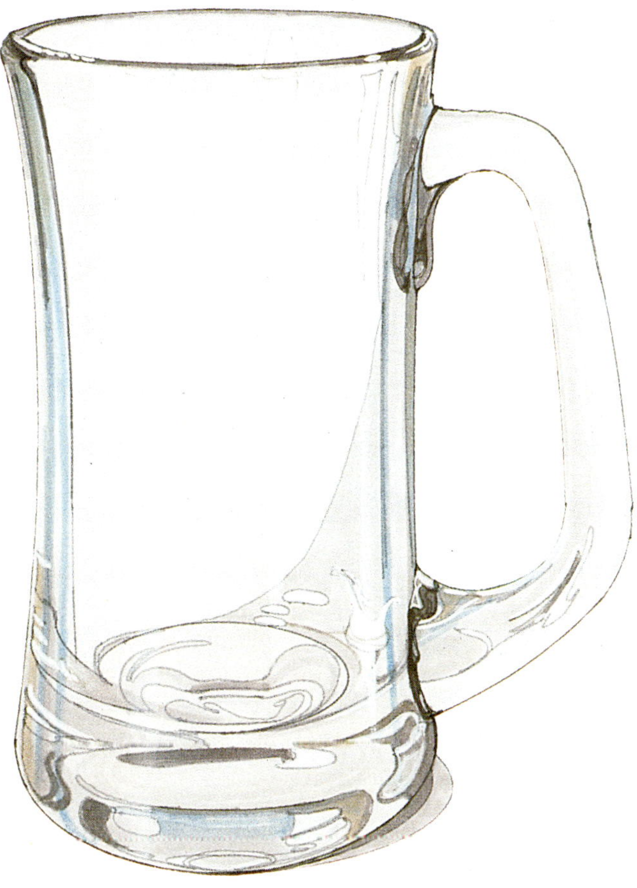

Step 4: 1) To show streaks of light on the surface, make vertical lines on the front of the glass using the fine point of a brick white marker. Then, stroke lines around the inside of the handle that complement its shape. 2) Fill in the cast shadow with a 40% gray. Use the broad nib to lay in this value. 3) Continue to develop the darks by stroking around the corners on the lip, the shapes near the bottom, and the place where the handle meets the glass with the fine point of a 70% gray marker.

Step 5: 1) Add the final darks to the corners on the lip and at the place where the handle is connected, using the fine point of a black marker. 2) To enhance the sense of dimension, apply 60% gray to the innermost part of the cast shadow. 3) Hard, white reflections are added with Dr. Martin's Bleed Proof White and a no. 0 sable brush. Start around the lip by dotting on paint near the corners. Next, paint the three highlights down the front, following the contour. Finally, use the drawing's guidelines to paint in the tiny shapes at the bottom.

PROJECT 1: *FINISHED ART*

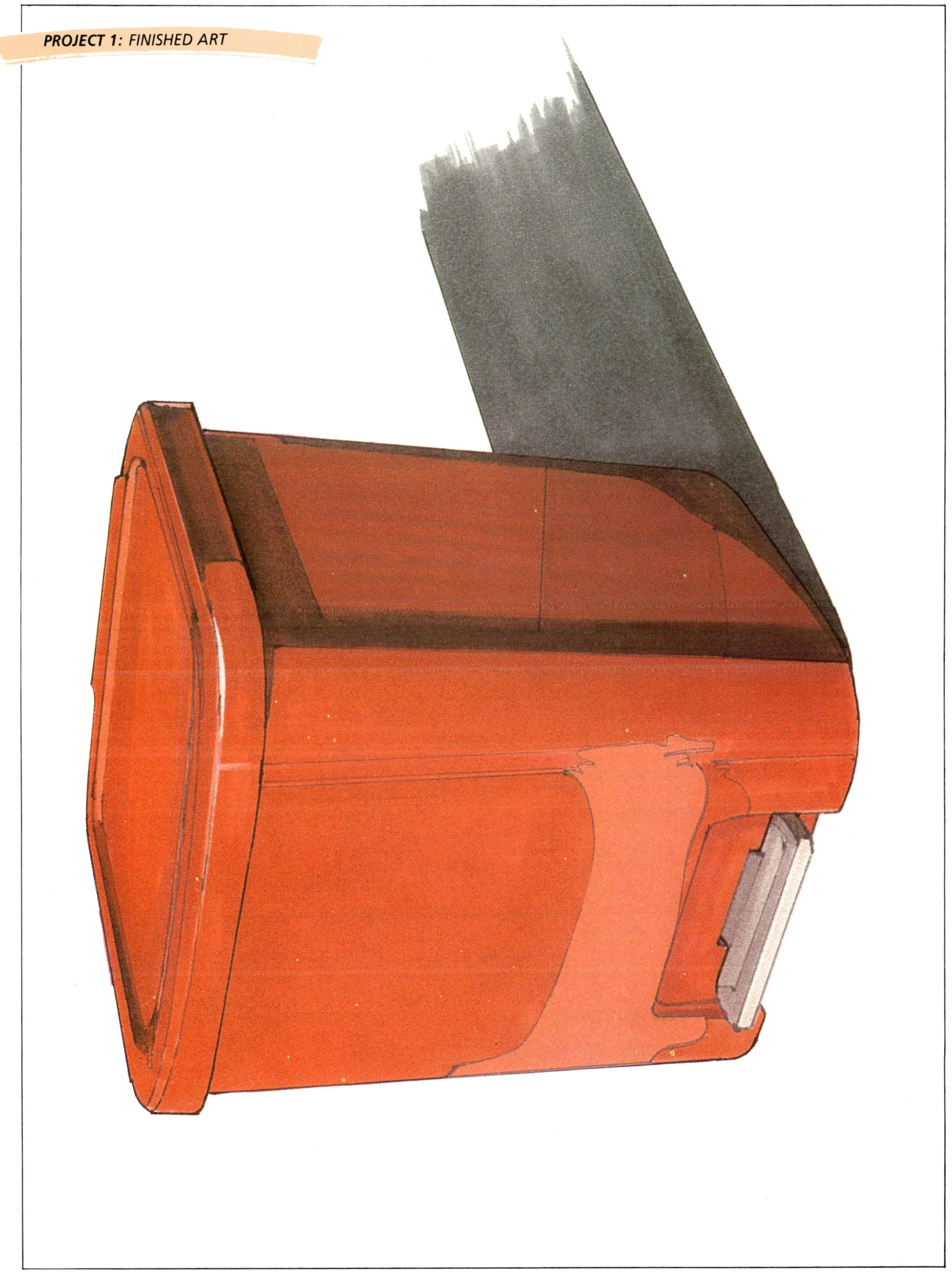

PROJECT 2: *FINISHED ART*

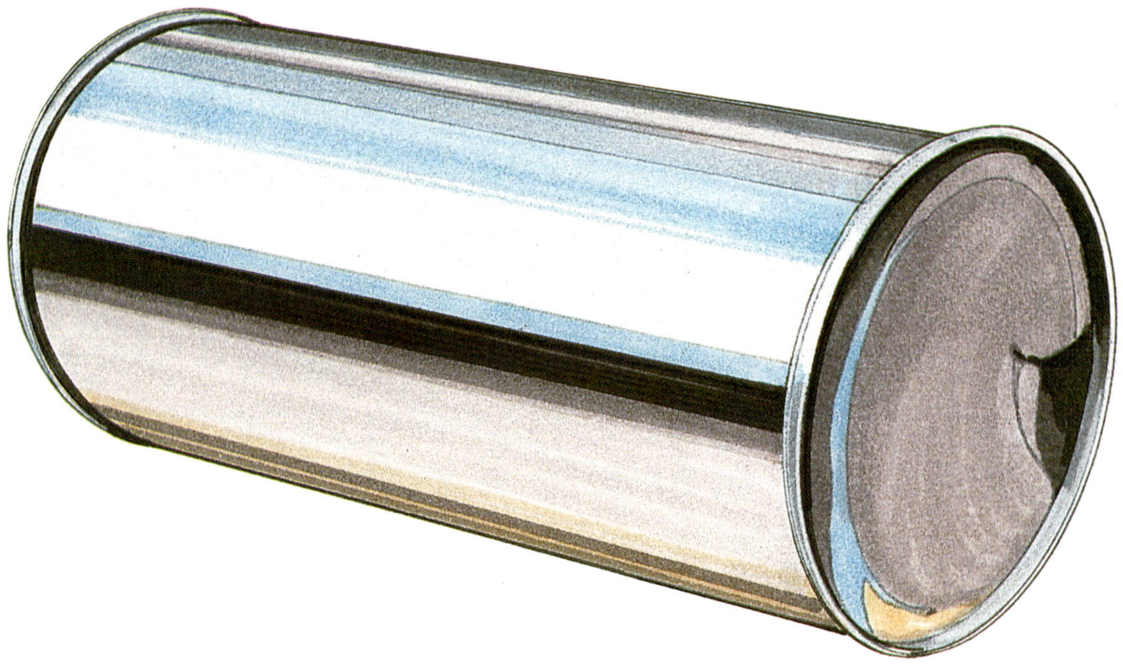

PROJECT 3: *FINISHED ART*

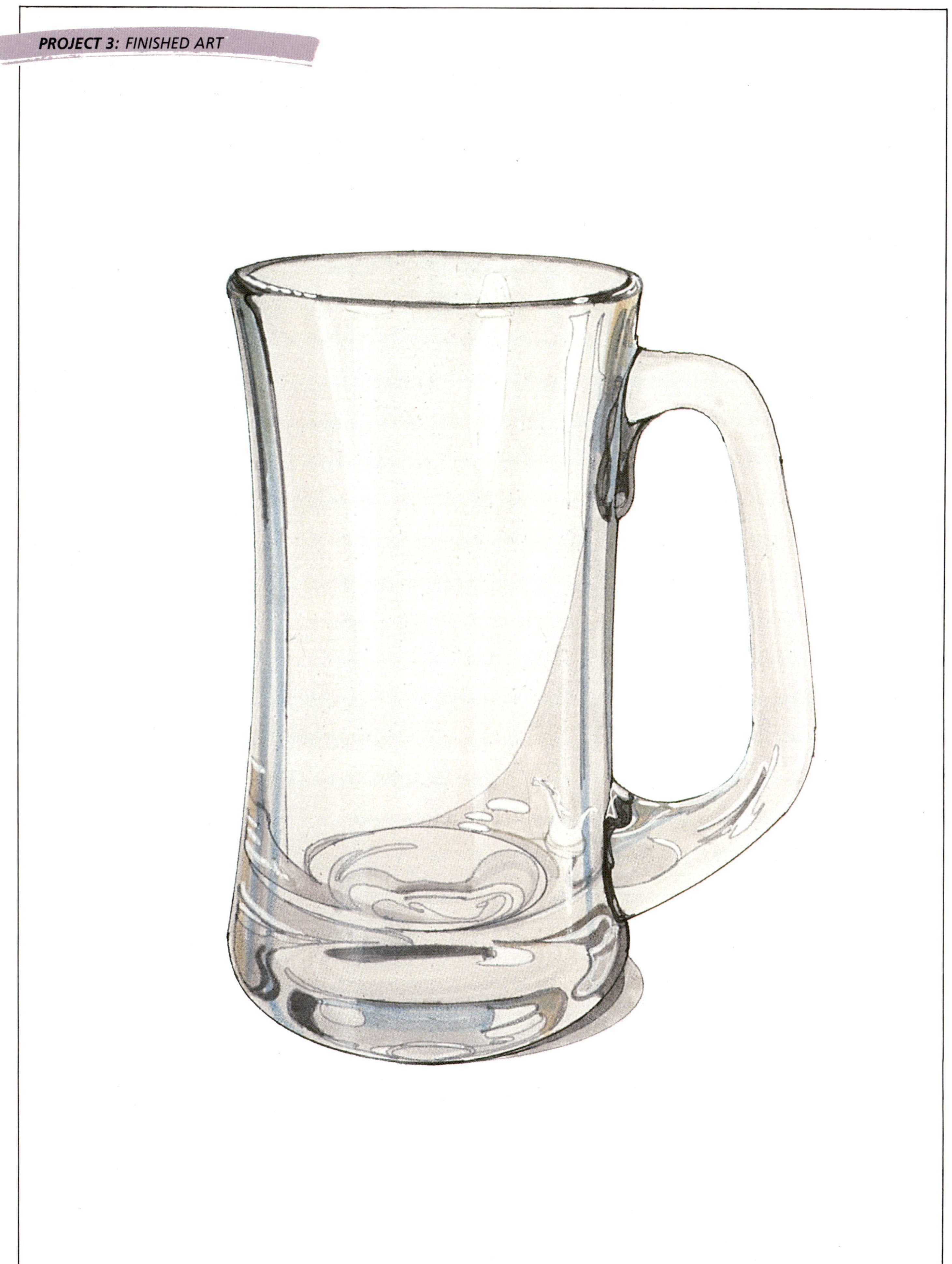

PROJECT 1: *PRACTICE*

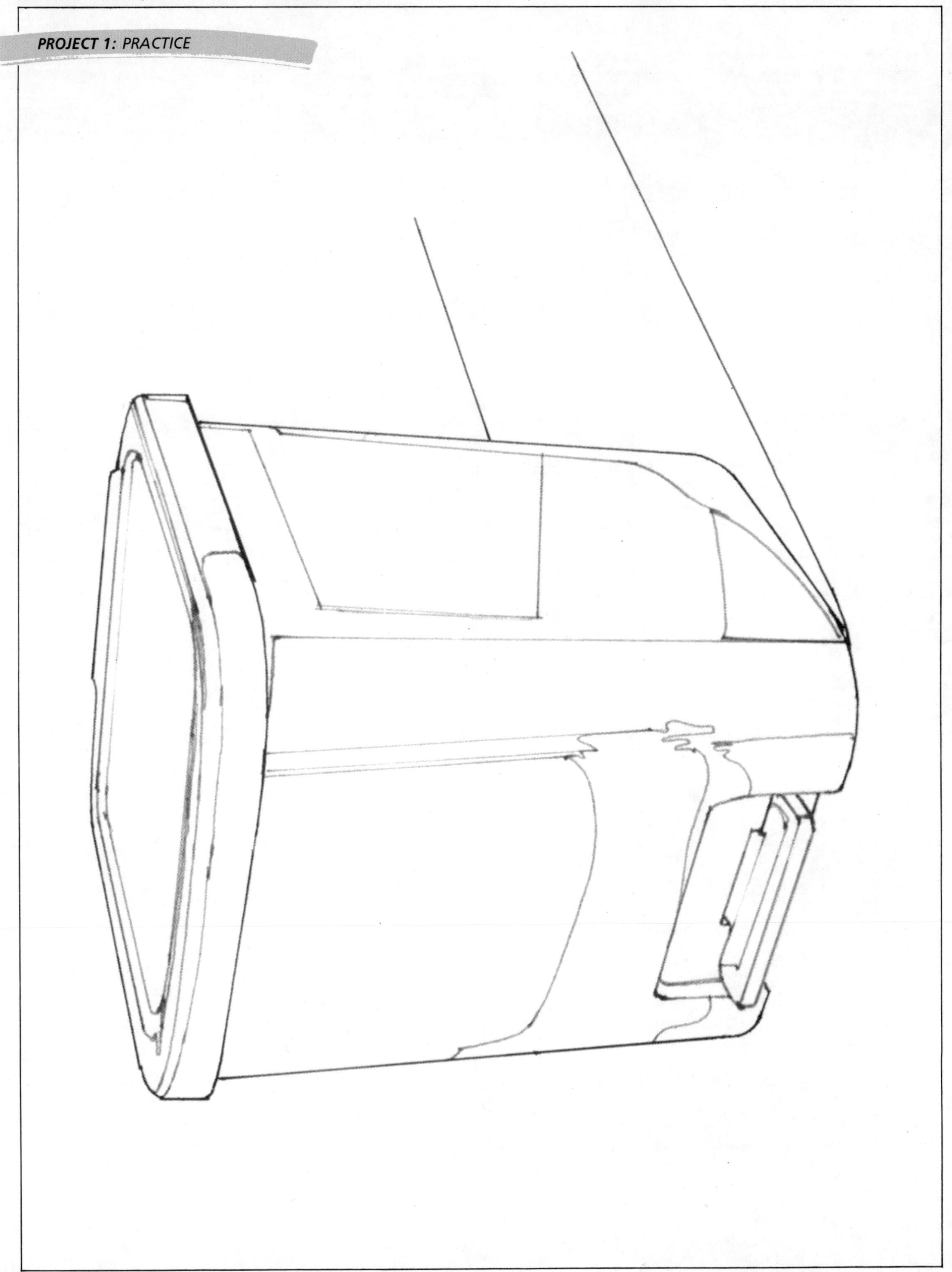

PROJECT 1: *PRACTICE*

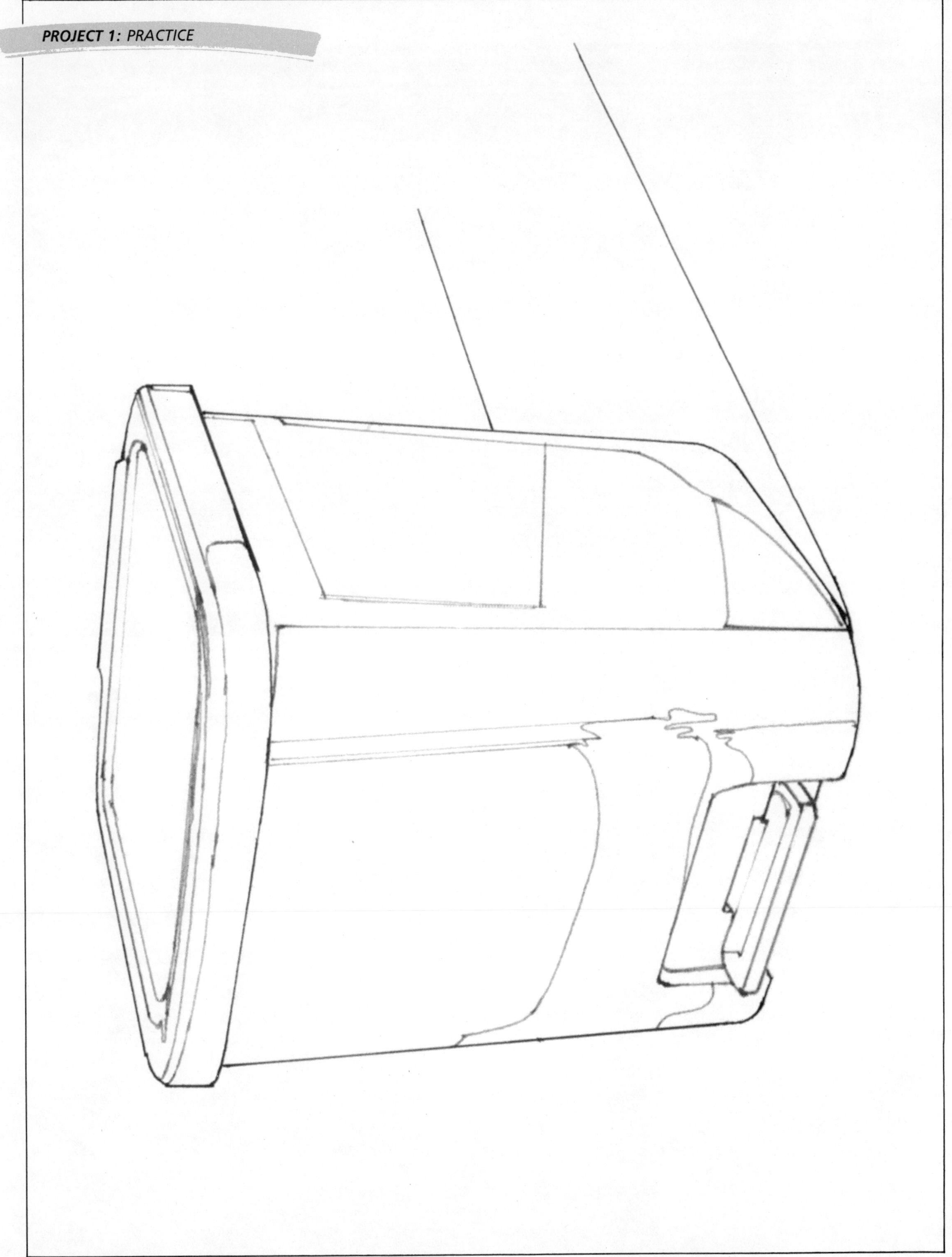

PROJECT 1: *PRACTICE*

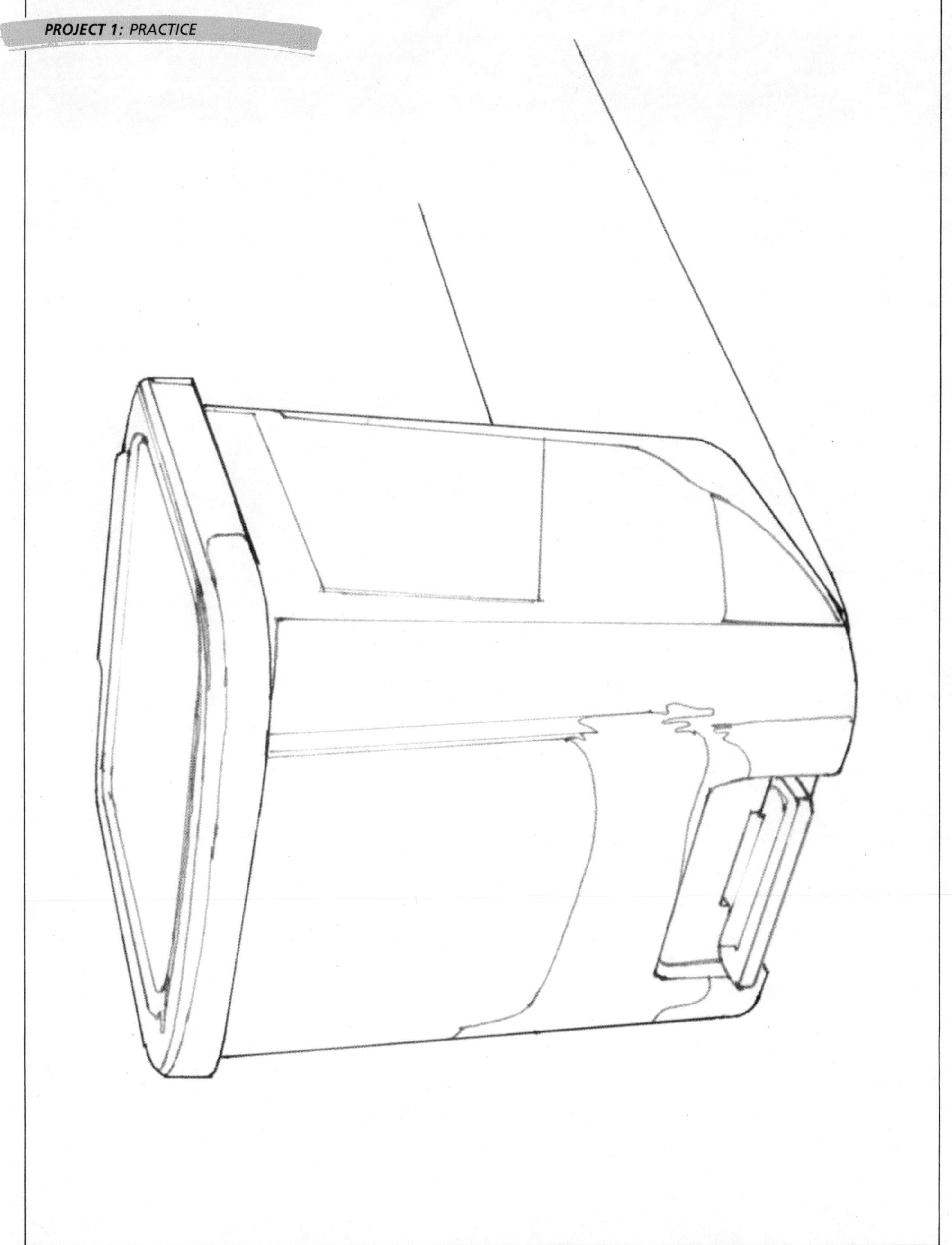

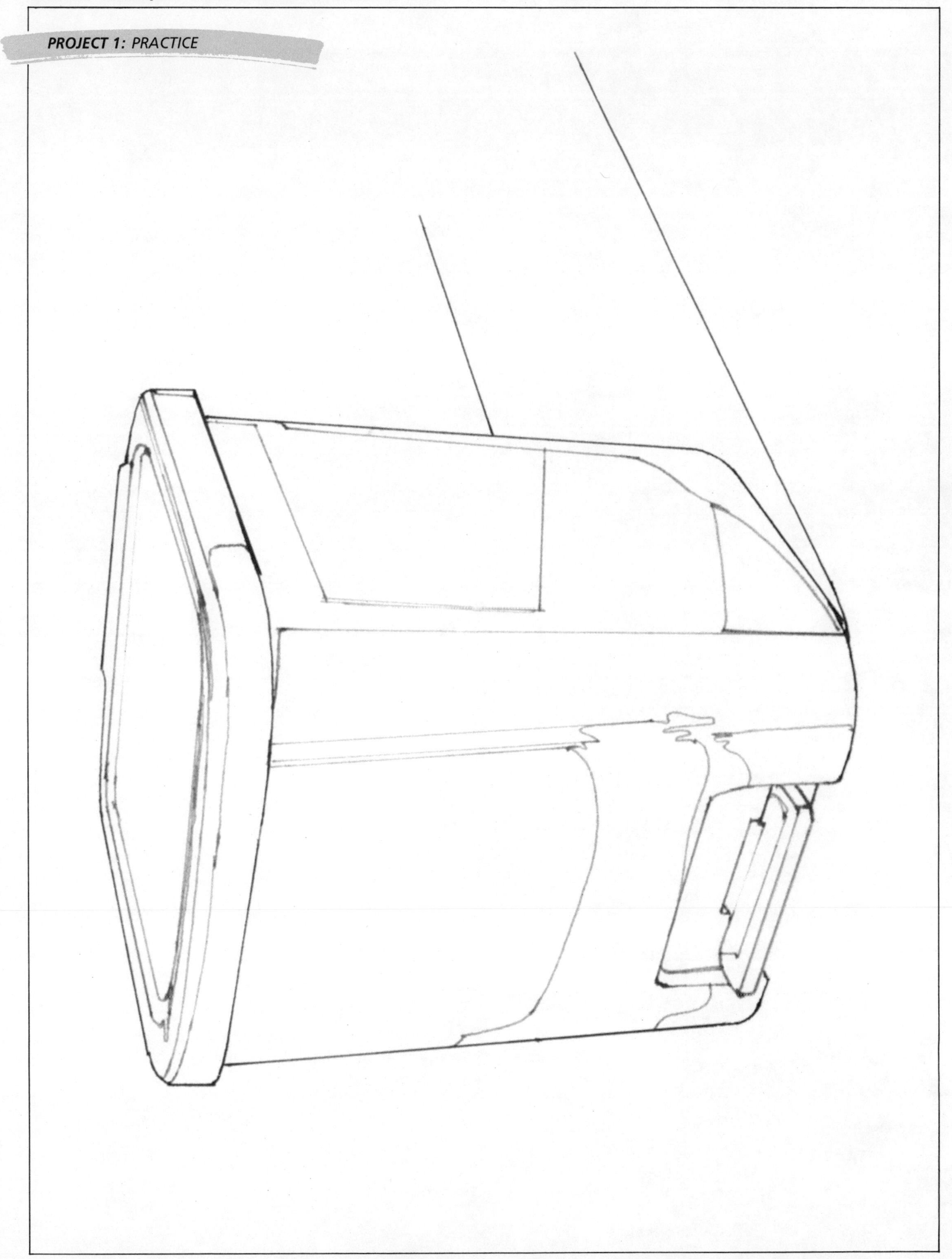

PROJECT 2: *PRACTICE*

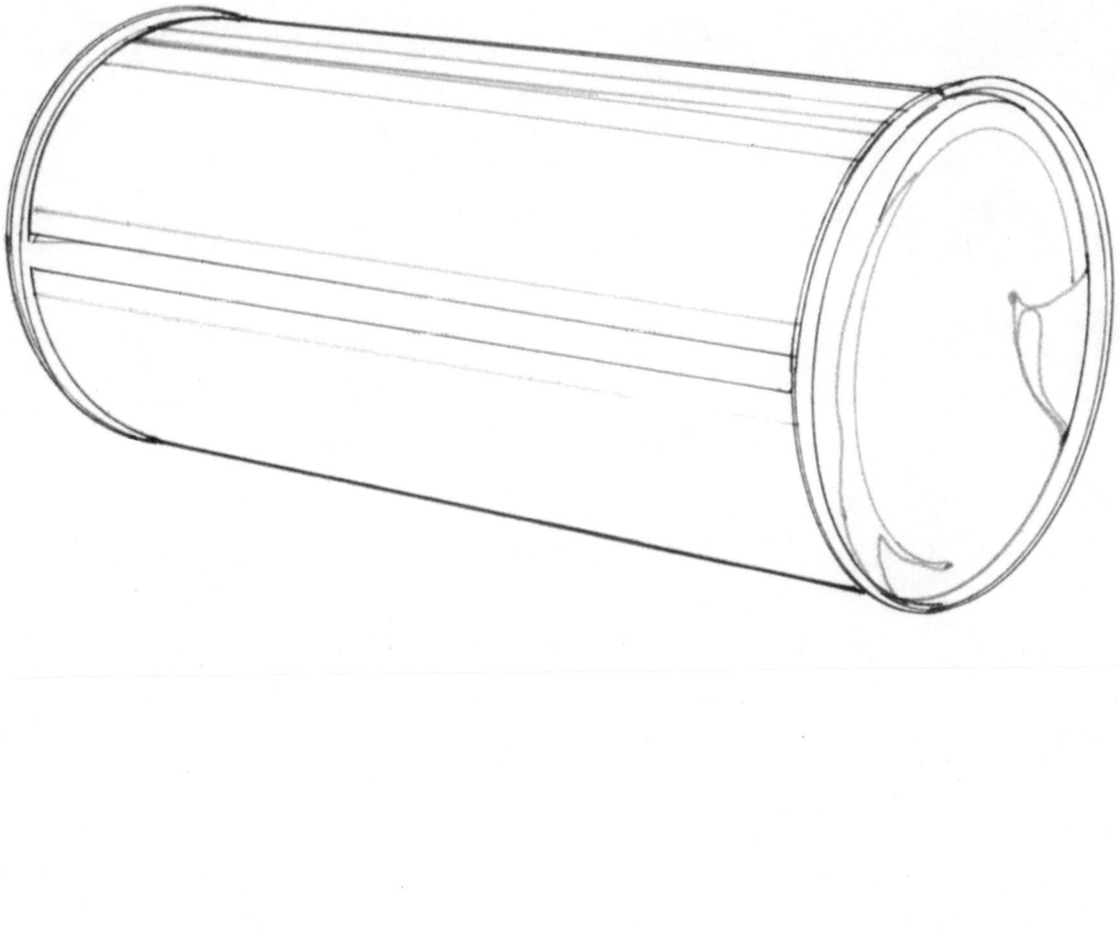

PROJECT 2: *PRACTICE*

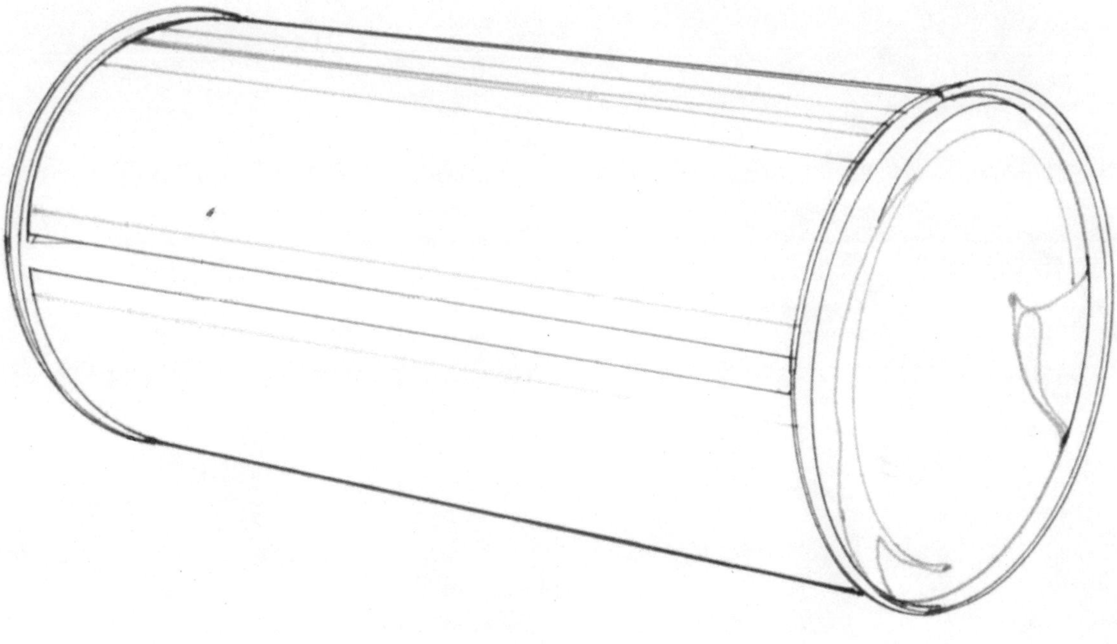

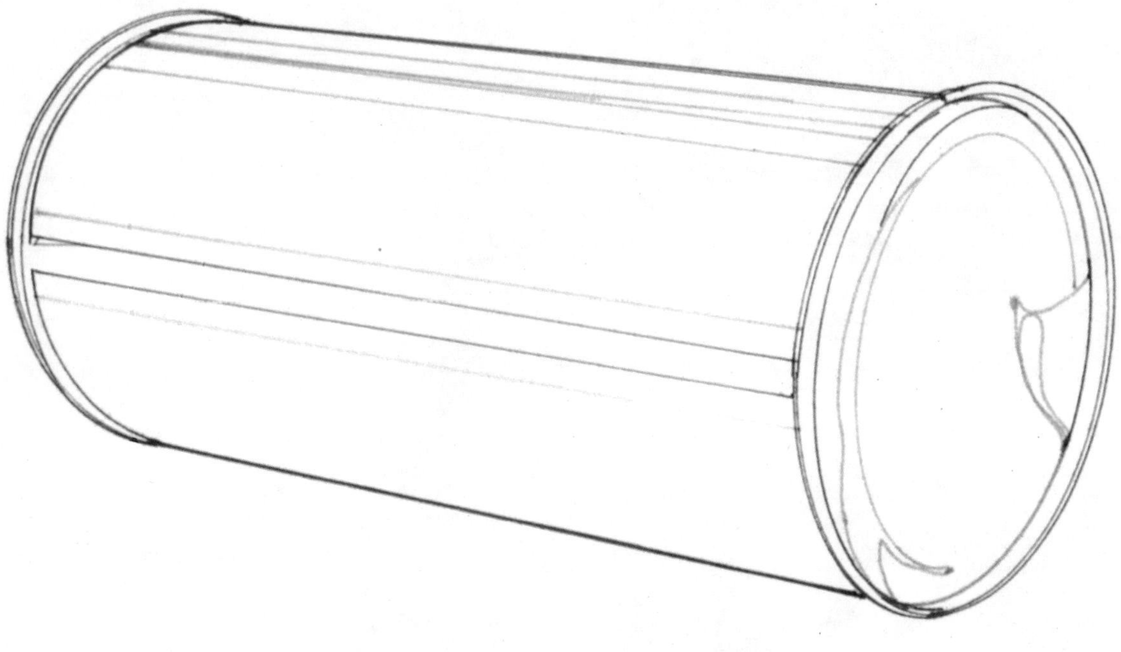

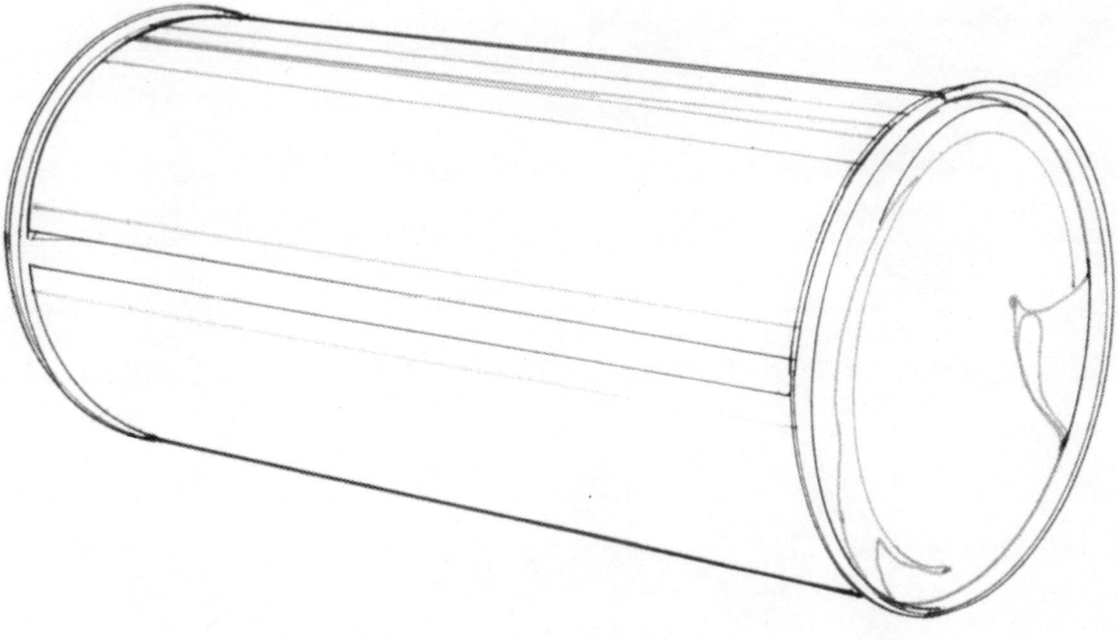

PROJECT 2: PRACTICE

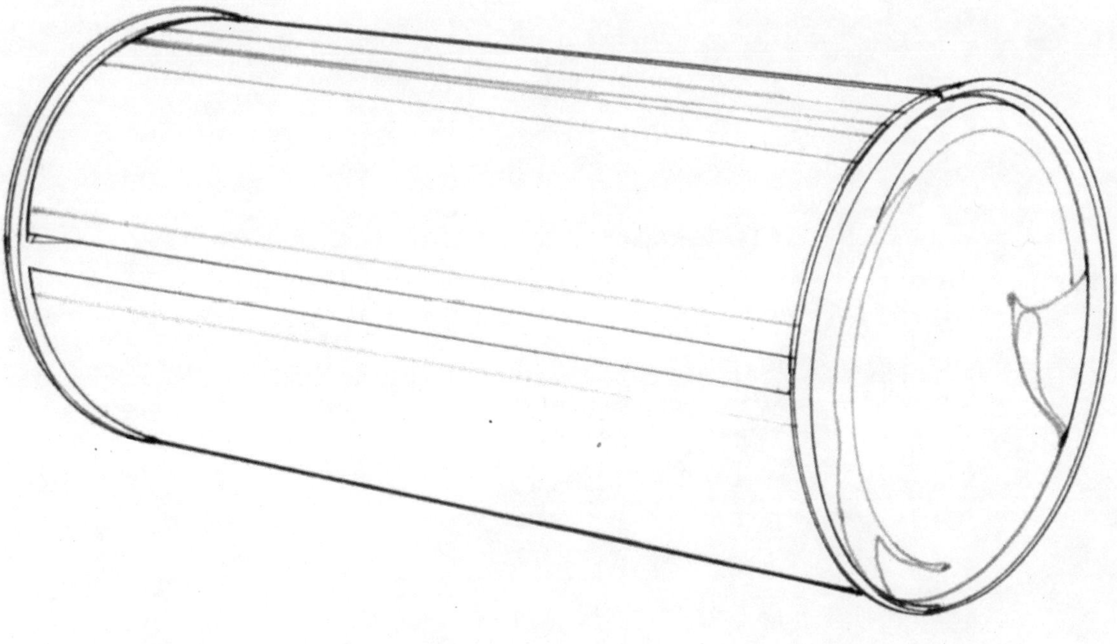

PROJECT 2: *PRACTICE*

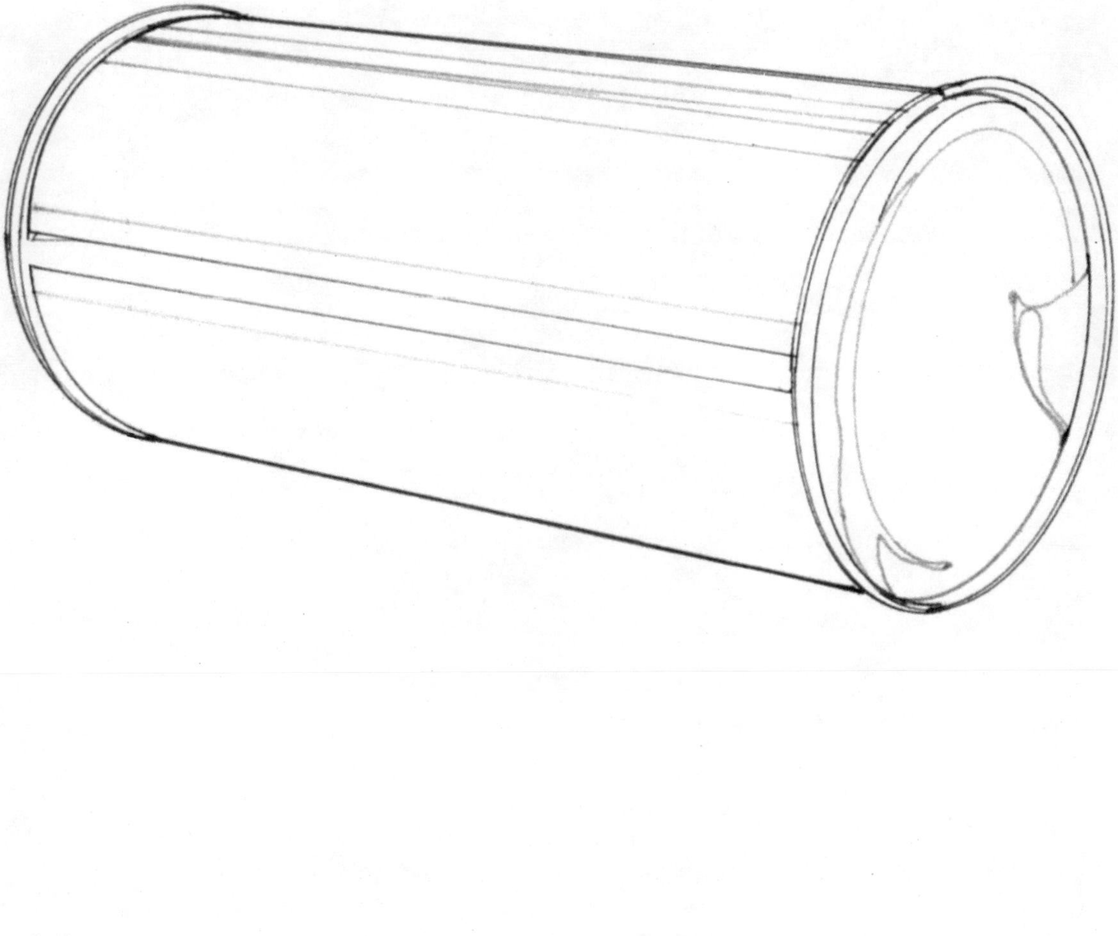

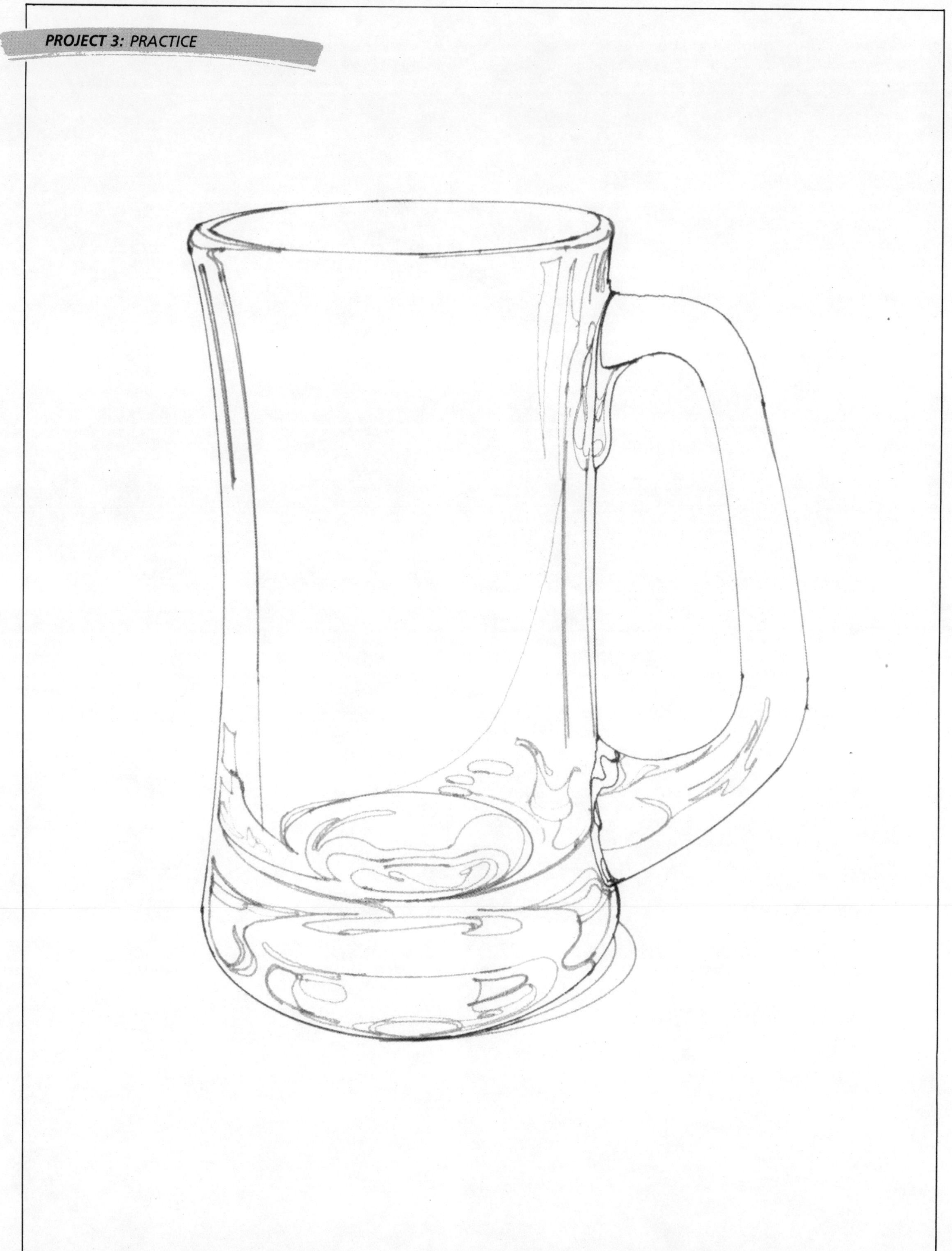

PROJECT 3: *PRACTICE*

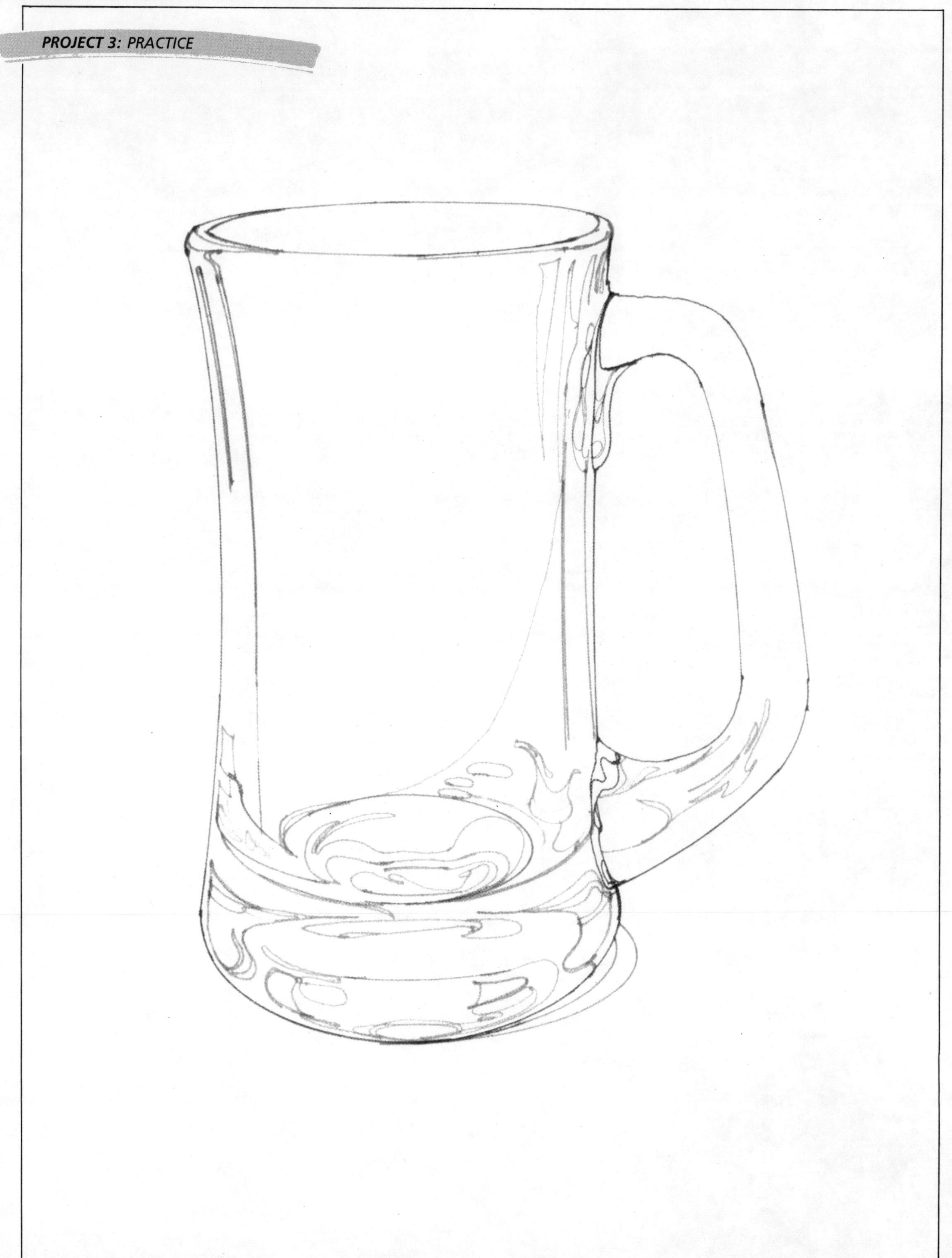

PROJECT 3: PRACTICE

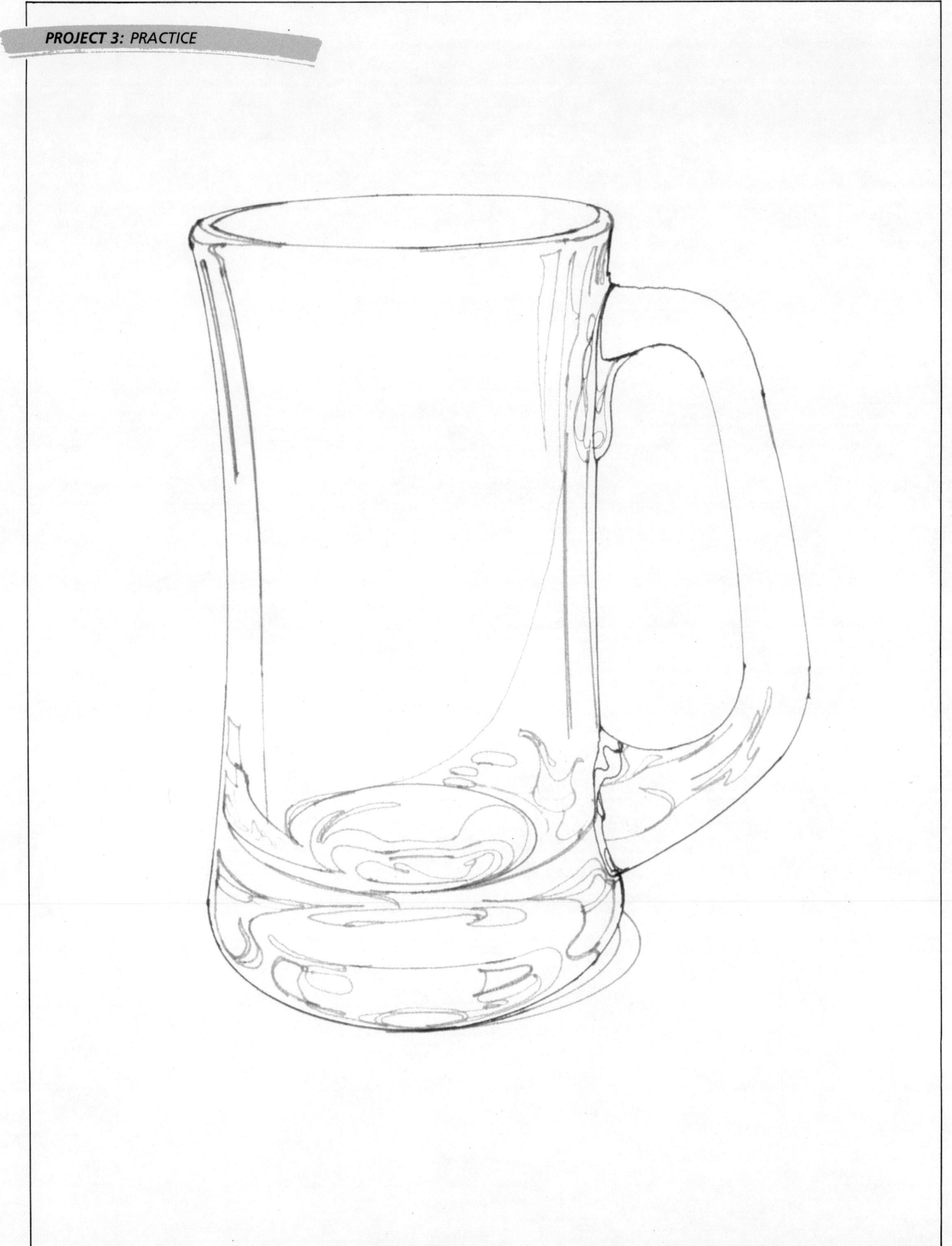

PROJECT 3: *PRACTICE*

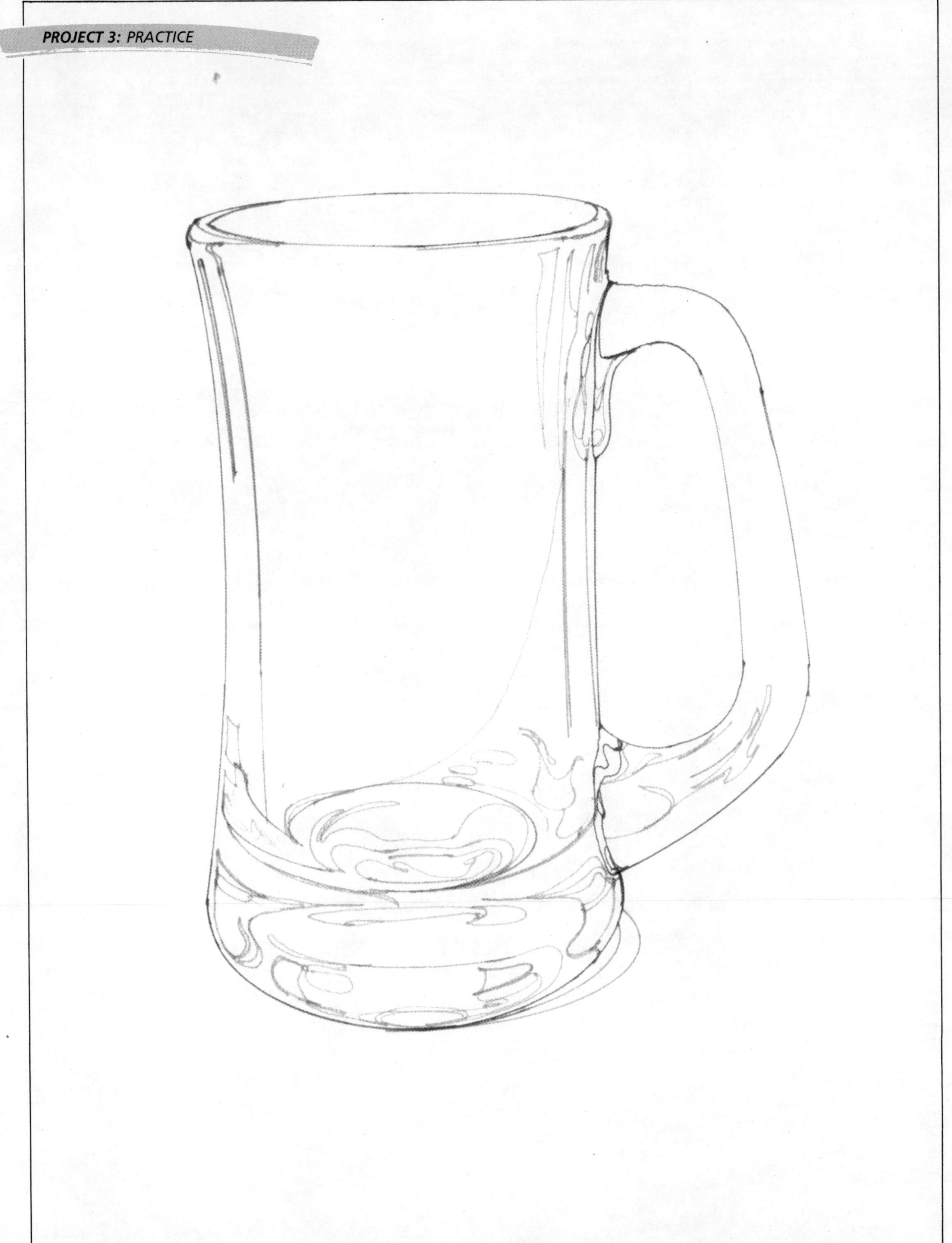

PROJECT 3: *PRACTICE*

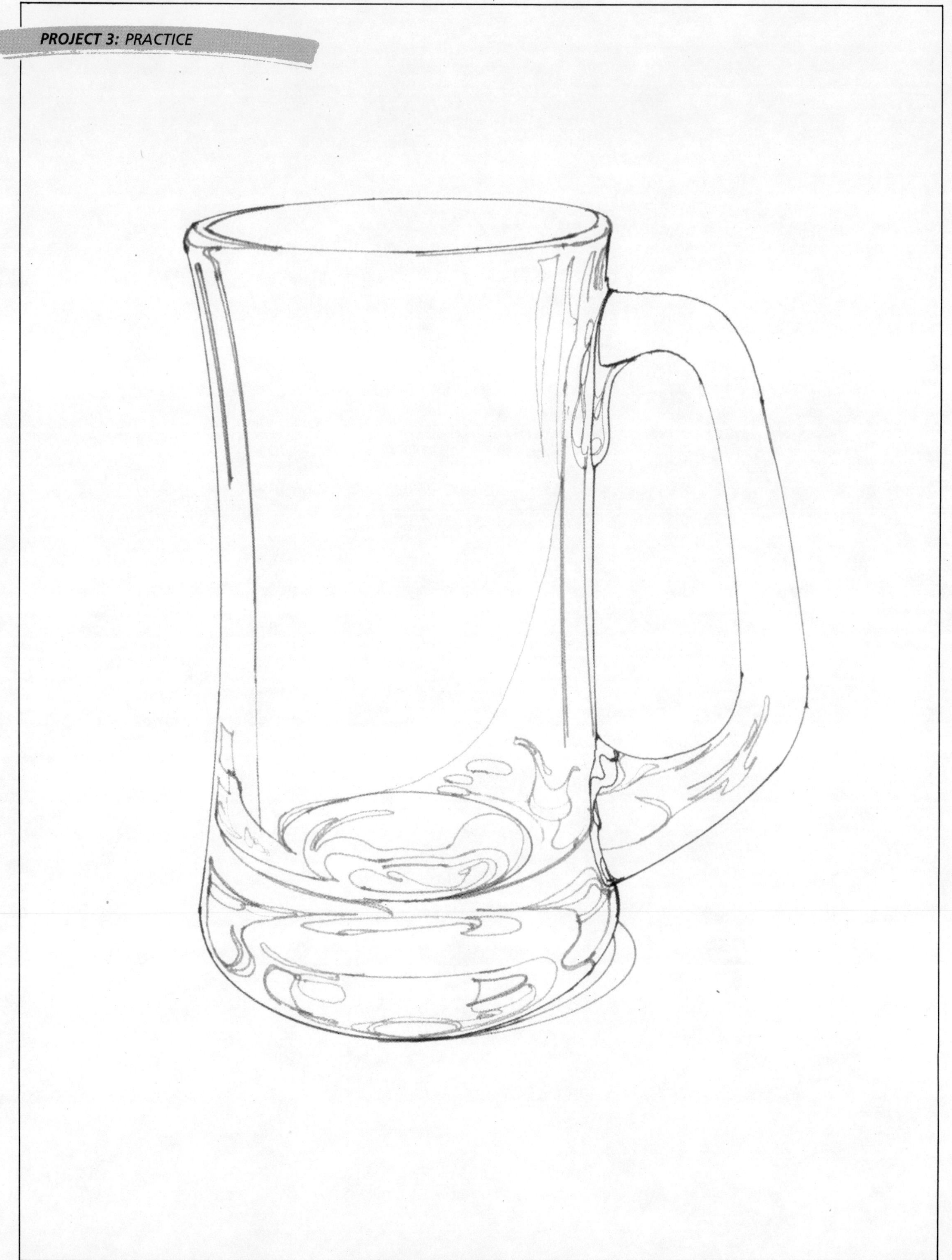

PROJECT 3: PRACTICE

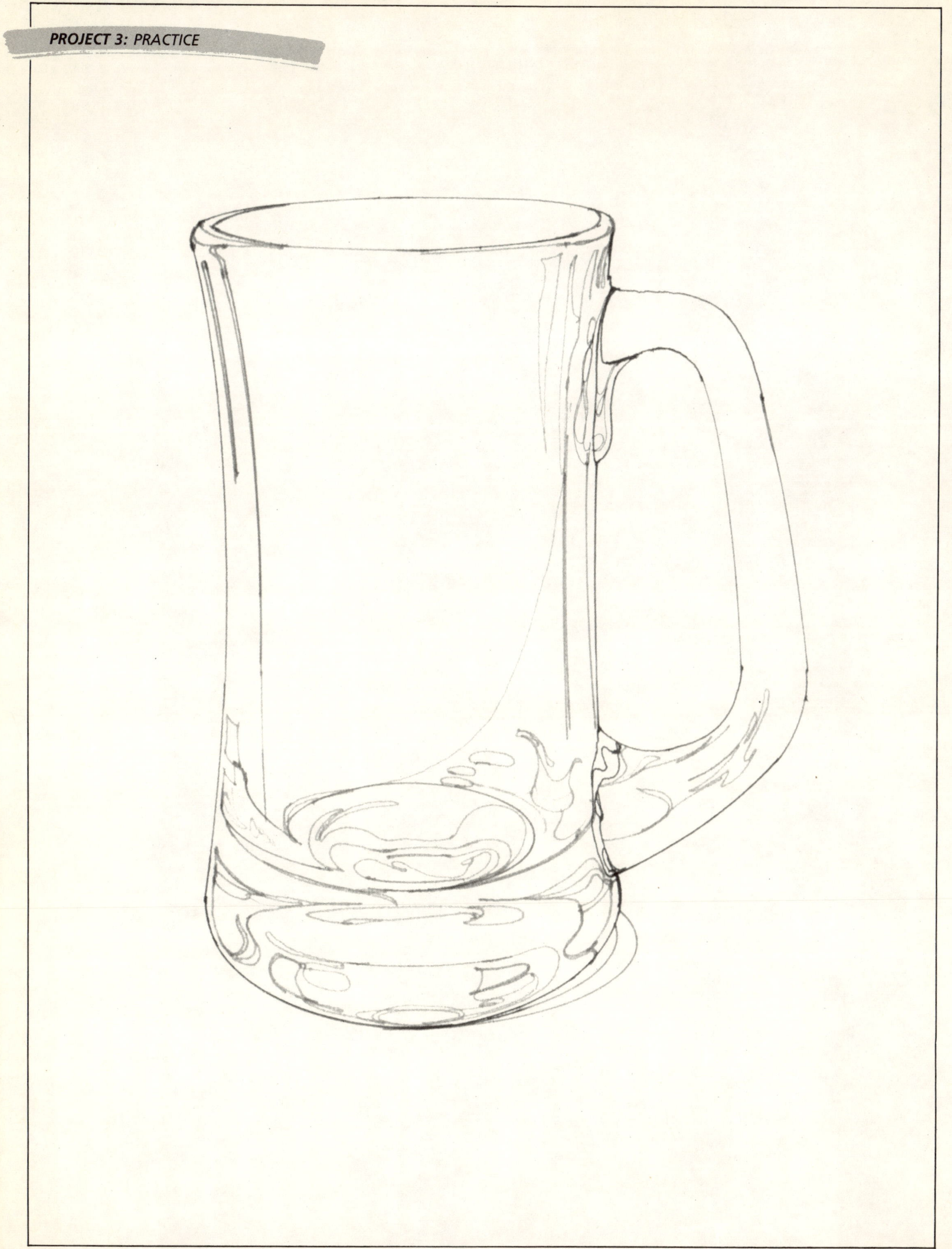